THE MUSIC THIEF

"In *The Music Thief,* Andy brings together two of his lifelong passions: playing music and standing up for what's right. The depth of his commitment to both finally bring him to an ethical conflict, and this is that story. It's a story that careens headlong from Andy's brutally punished longhair protest of the Vietnam War in grade school, to his days learning to improvise and perform on several instruments and in theater, to his years of peregrination around the world, pursuing his music and working day jobs, trespassing on different cultures, finally winding up in the end back where he started. And there, confronting his ethical dilemma head on, he solves the puzzle of the life he wants to live and the man he wants to be. This is a story about justice, in the end. And an existential moment."—Rick Hendra, host of *Seeds and Stems,* WCUW Community Radio/Worcester; Professor (retired), University Without Walls at University of Massachusetts, Amherst

"Andy Laties had the good fortune to be raised by progressive parents who encouraged his rebelliousness, his creativity, his idealism. And he had the misfortune to step out into a world that had little use for his rebelliousness, his creativity, or his idealism. *The Music Thief* is Andy's lucid and wise coming-of-age memoir, in which the author searches for himself in the worlds of improvisational theater, free jazz, and Black liberation. But his explorations lead to a head-on collision with reality when he hears someone yelling, 'Help, murder! Help! They're killing me!'"—Seth Tobocman, *You Don't Have to Fuck People Over to Survive;* co-founder *World War 3 Illustrated*

Praise for *Rebel Bookseller: Why Indie Businesses Represent Everything You Want to Fight For—From Free Speech to Buying Local to Building Communities*

"A must-read"—*Publishers Weekly* (starred review)

"Everything you always wanted to know about the book business but were afraid to ask."—Eric Carle, *The Very Hungry Caterpillar*

"Laties is witty, opinionated for sure, impassioned, but eminently practical in both his desires for independent bookselling and how to actually do it effectively. Activists of all stripes, not just booksellers, can learn from this book. It made me laugh. It made me think. It inspired me. It'll do the same for you too."—Ramsey Kanaan, co-founder AK Press and PM Press

Praise for *Son of Rebel Bookseller: A Very Large Homework Assignment:*

"Interlaced with the vivid imaginative writing Samuel Laties composed throughout his short life, *Son of Rebel Bookseller* is a testament to a father's love for his son and a chronicle of the search for meaning after devastating loss. It's also the story of a father's heroic efforts, despite the weight of grief, to save a bookstore and to create dynamic and memorable in-store performances for children. This poignant account testifies in support of one of the most profound ways we can cherish our children: by inspiring their imaginations."—Lee Upton, *The Tao of Humiliation: Stories*

"An intimate, heart-rending memoir."—Julie Corsaro, Past President, Association for Library Service to Children

THE MUSIC THIEF

a memoir

ANDREW LATIES

Copyright © 2020 by Andrew Laties

All rights reserved. No part of this book may be reproduced, stored in a retrieval system, or transmitted in any form, or by any means, including mechanical, electric, photocopying, recording, or otherwise, without the prior written permission of the copyright owner.

Cataloging in Publication Data
Laties, Andrew
 The music thief: a memoir / Andrew Laties

ISBN 978-1-953465-00-9 (pbk.)
ISBN 978-1-953465-01-6 (ebook)

1. Musicians—United States
2. Race and Ethnic Relations
3. Biography & Autobiography
4. Laties, Andrew

The events and conversations in this book have been set down to the best of the author's ability.

Front jacket: *Portrait of Andy Laties* by Mary Phelan,

Cover design by Rebecca Migdal

Printed and bound in the United States of America

First printing September 1, 2020
Published by Mythoprint Publishing
Easton, PA, USA, 18042

For Mom

"Congress shall make no law respecting an establishment of religion, or prohibiting the free exercise thereof; or abridging the freedom of speech, or of the press; or the right of the people peaceably to assemble, and to petition the Government for a redress of grievances."

—*First Amendment, United States Constitution*

Contents

PROLOGUE—BLACK AND WHITE 1

1-SIXTIES KID 5

2-IN AND OUT AT YALE 31

3-GOING TO CHICAGO 51

4-THERE AND BACK AGAIN 69

5-REFUGEES IN PARIS 97

6-RETURNING THE FAVOR 109

POSTSCRIPT 119

ACKNOWLEDGMENTS 123

NOTES 125

PROLOGUE—BLACK AND WHITE

APRIL 2012

"Are you George?"

I had dashed past the distinguished customer while he browsed, then done a double take.

"Yes. Do we know each other?"

I'd started a month before as manager at Park Place Bookstore, on the Upper West Side of Manhattan.

"The last place I saw you was Chicago, in AACM School—thirty years ago. You had one kid calling out the colors of passing cars, while another played the piano notes assigned to each color."

"I did that?"

I was stunned to be chatting so casually with this man who with his 1977 *George Lewis Solo Trombone Record* had inspired my youthful Association for the Advancement of Creative Musicians (AACM) odyssey.

"And, I had caught you in Paris, the year before—with Derek Bailey."

Uh-oh. He had zero memory of me.

I gamely continued, "I studied with Douglas Ewart."

Now we were on terra firma. "You know Douglas? He's one of my closest friends—I saw him a few months ago."

"How's he doing? Wait—just a second." I darted to the office and dug out a scrapbook from my years at The Children's Bookstore. I'd brought it in to show my twentysomething employees. I flipped through, located what I needed, slipped this from its protective sleeve, and returned to the sales floor.

"Take a look." George examined the photo of Douglas Ewart playing flute, flanked by a young drummer and three other child instrumentalists. "That's the AACM School Small Ensemble, performing in my bookstore, in 1986."

He was smiling. "I'm looking for a book for my son. Can you recommend something for a seven-year-old?"

An hour later, when I looked up George Lewis on the Internet, I saw I'd lost track of his career. He was an endowed professor at Columbia University, a few blocks away. He'd received a MacArthur Fellowship. And, in 2008, he'd published a scholarly history of the AACM, called *A Power Stronger than Itself: The AACM and American Experimental Music*.

I ordered a copy.

This thick book was eye-opening. I found myself skipping halfway through, to where the early eighties were covered. Wow, I'd had no idea what was happening behind the scenes.

I read the whole thing. Interesting: Bob Dogan—a white piano player—had been invited in 1965 to AACM's third meeting, to attend but not to join. An audiotape transcript documented co-founder Muhal Richard Abrams explaining that one benefit of convening an all-Black group would be to support healthier interracial collaboration: "We're not fighting a racial fight. We're promoting ourselves and helping ourselves up to the point where we can participate in the universal aspect of things, which includes all people."

Throughout the book, oral history was unbelievably thorough. Additional research analyzed dozens of never-before-translated articles from European jazz magazines; these ranged from the sublime to the ridiculous. (In fact, the entire opus was laced with dry wit.) The capstone was a remarkable imaginary conversation, a ten-page "unstable polyphony of quoted voices, a kind of virtual AACM meeting." There, I read these frank, Black-power-inflected comments—which built on Muhal Richard Abrams' "includes all people" comment to Bob Dogan:

> [Kelan said], "It's my thinking that music is the language of a people, and I was interested in what the language could do for black people. I wasn't interested in what it could do for whites."
> …Maia was pensive. "Racism has not gone away. We have more opportunities in some ways and we have less in other ways."
> …"Our idea of bringing the AACM together was to control our destiny as a people," Sparx said. …"That was predicated on what has happened in the past to a lot of artists, in terms of their creations, and what they got from that materially."

This highly-charged white-theft-of-Black-music narrative—and my evolving understanding of it—had shaped my life. Over the years, I'd heard various white musician friends protest that it was an unfair cliché. I had never before encountered so many nuanced analyses from varying Black perspectives. Then—I was looking in the mirror:

> "For a while," Ann reminded everyone, "the AACM School had white faculty and students, which was considered problematic by some members."

> That was me: "white…student…problematic."

1-SIXTIES KID

APRIL 4, 1968

Martin Luther King Shot… Martin Luther King Shot… Martin Luther King Shot…. The words were scrolling over my Bugs Bunny cartoon. I got Daddy. He was upset.

A week later, we went to a church concert for Martin Luther King. I sat on the floor, in front of four men playing fast music on huge golden saxophones. A woman sang, "I been to the mountaintop / Hail the justice of the Lord."

I didn't know much about Martin Luther King, but the concert was so good that I felt something important was happening that I was a part of, and I wanted to be more a part of.

I began to learn about the Civil Rights movement. From a flat box, Mommy took out pictures by Ben Shaun, showing Chaney, Goodman and Schwerner. Andrew Goodman and Michael Schwerner were Jewish like us; their friend James Chaney was Black. They were killed by the Ku Klux Klan, during Freedom Summer, in Mississippi, for helping Black people vote.

*   *   *

Mommy said nobody should make kids say prayers in school. She ran MCPEARL—Monroe Citizens for Public Education and Religious Liberty—which told congress it should be public funds for public schools only. On her wall was a framed plaque of the First Amendment. When she wrote newsletters, there were parties with her friends stapling pages and stuffing envelopes. If I did it too, I got a penny an envelope.

Mommy was an atheist, so I was too. One night at bedtime I told her I was worried that after I died, God might be mad at me for not believing in him. She recited a poem:

> Abou Ben Adhem (may his tribe increase!)
> Awoke one night from a deep dream of peace,
> And saw, within the moonlight in his room,
> Making it rich, and like a lily in bloom,
> An angel writing in a book of gold:—
> Exceeding peace had made Ben Adhem bold,
> And to the presence in the room he said,
> "What writest thou?"—The vision raised its head,
> And with a look made of all sweet accord,
> Answered, "The names of those who love the Lord."
> "And is mine one?" said Abou. "Nay, not so,"
> Replied the angel. Abou spoke more low,
> But cheerily still; and said, "I pray thee, then,
> Write me as one that loves his fellow men."

1-SIXTIES KID

APRIL 4, 1968

Martin Luther King Shot… Martin Luther King Shot… Martin Luther King Shot…. The words were scrolling over my Bugs Bunny cartoon. I got Daddy. He was upset.

A week later, we went to a church concert for Martin Luther King. I sat on the floor, in front of four men playing fast music on huge golden saxophones. A woman sang, "I been to the mountaintop / Hail the justice of the Lord."

I didn't know much about Martin Luther King, but the concert was so good that I felt something important was happening that I was a part of, and I wanted to be more a part of.

I began to learn about the Civil Rights movement. From a flat box, Mommy took out pictures by Ben Shaun, showing Chaney, Goodman and Schwerner. Andrew Goodman and Michael Schwerner were Jewish like us; their friend James Chaney was Black. They were killed by the Ku Klux Klan, during Freedom Summer, in Mississippi, for helping Black people vote.

* * *

Mommy said nobody should make kids say prayers in school. She ran MCPEARL—Monroe Citizens for Public Education and Religious Liberty—which told congress it should be public funds for public schools only. On her wall was a framed plaque of the First Amendment. When she wrote newsletters, there were parties with her friends stapling pages and stuffing envelopes. If I did it too, I got a penny an envelope.

Mommy was an atheist, so I was too. One night at bedtime I told her I was worried that after I died, God might be mad at me for not believing in him. She recited a poem:

> Abou Ben Adhem (may his tribe increase!)
> Awoke one night from a deep dream of peace,
> And saw, within the moonlight in his room,
> Making it rich, and like a lily in bloom,
> An angel writing in a book of gold:—
> Exceeding peace had made Ben Adhem bold,
> And to the presence in the room he said,
> "What writest thou?"—The vision raised its head,
> And with a look made of all sweet accord,
> Answered, "The names of those who love the Lord."
> "And is mine one?" said Abou. "Nay, not so,"
> Replied the angel. Abou spoke more low,
> But cheerily still; and said, "I pray thee, then,
> Write me as one that loves his fellow men."

The angel wrote, and vanished. The next night
It came again with a great wakening light,
And showed the names whom love of God had blest,
And lo! Ben Adhem's name led all the rest.

There was starvation in Biafra. TV showed children whose stomachs stuck way out. I asked if I could donate some of my allowance. CARE sent mail with pictures of kids I was helping.

Every night at dinner we watched the six o'clock news with Walter Cronkite. It was the Vietnam War, direct from the battlefield: helicopters, guns, explosions; villagers and soldiers wounded and killed.
    Walter Cronkite started by saying how many: "One-thousand-four-hundred-and-twenty North Vietnamese dead. Eight-hundred-and-seventy-one Viet Cong dead. One-hundred-and-nineteen South Vietnamese dead. Forty-two Americans dead." The numbers were always in the same order, and they showed a lot more people on the North Vietnamese side were being killed than on the South Vietnamese, so our side was winning. I didn't know how so many Vietnamese could be killed but more could still be left.
    There were interviews with American generals about how the US Army was keeping the North Vietnamese out of South Vietnam. The problem was the Viet Cong. These were communists who lived in South Vietnam. They fought by sneaking out of tunnels and killing Americans from behind.

One time, Walter Cronkite said the war wasn't going right. It was different, that night when he told what he really thought. My family agreed: Mommy wanted Gene McCarthy for president, so we'd get out of Vietnam.

As 1968 went on—with the assassination of Robert Kennedy, who was on our side of civil rights, and then, with the anti-war protests at the Chicago Democratic Convention, where police beat up long-haired students—I developed strong opinions about who I was in the world.

That summer, I grew my hair long against the Vietnam War. By the time I started fourth grade this protest had made me look like a girl and earned me the insult, "Laties is a lady," and the names homo and faggot. Some kids did ask why my hair was long; when I said I was protesting the Vietnam War, they yelled I was a commie hippie.

On the school bus, kids would call me out, saying I had to meet them in the woods. I'd refuse because I was in favor of peace. They'd call me a sissy.

At one point, I counted forty-eight nasty nicknames. When they'd start in, I'd rattle off all the names they'd invented back in their faces. I'd say I was reminding them, so they wouldn't skip any.

I also worked out a way of staring at them without blinking—like Max in *Where the Wild Things Are*. No matter what they said, I'd keep staring.

The other boys wouldn't let me play baseball, but they did make me permanent catcher. One afternoon someone yelled, "The kid who gets the last out gets pantsed." I didn't know what this meant. When there were two outs in the bottom of the ninth, they handed me the bat and said, "Okay Laties, if you get a hit you don't have to be permanent catcher anymore."

I struck out. They yelled, "Get him!" I ran through the trees, but they caught me. Five kids held me to the ground while two others pulled off my pants and underwear. I was sobbing and yelling. They laughed and left.

When I told Mom kids were teasing me and I didn't know what to do, she said, "He that fights and runs away lives to fight another day."

I missed the bus and Mom had to drive me to school, so I was late. As I hurried down the empty hallway, Mr. Lazenby was coming from the opposite direction. He squatted, stared into my eyes, and said, "Hmm, green—I guess you'll be with the blue-eyes group." I'd always thought I had blue eyes, but it was true that they were a little green. Anyway, I didn't know what he was talking about and he said it was a surprise, and I'd better get to class.

When I went in, I saw that many of the kids were sitting in different desks than usual. Mr. Lazenby came back and said I could sit in my regular desk. Then he started talking about how, now that all the kids with brown eyes were on one side of the room, and all the kids with blue eyes were on the other side, he would tell us what unusual thing would be going on this day.

We were going to learn about discrimination. All day, the kids with blue eyes would have a normal day. But the kids with brown eyes would have to wait to do everything until the blue-eyed kids were finished. So, the brown-eyed kids would wait to have lunch until after blue-eyed kids were finished. And the brown-eyed kids wouldn't go to recess but would have to stay inside. Also, they wouldn't be allowed to use the regular school bathroom. They'd have to wait until just before lunch and then line up outside the nurse's one-toilet bathroom.

Tomorrow, it would be the blue-eyed kids' turns to experience discrimination.

I thought it was interesting that with my green eyes, I didn't belong in either group.

My day with the blue-eyed kids was normal, and I didn't notice much about what was going on with the brown-eyeds. Maybe things were a little faster for me in the lunch line, that was about it. However, Phil Heinrich, who had lived down the street from me back in first grade, but then moved away, was in the brown-eyed group. I didn't see much of him that day, but at the end, as we were leaving, I realized he was crying hard. Phil was usually energetic. He was good at all sports and games and had lots of friends. I'd never seen him cry. I was amazed he was so sad, just from having to wait in line to go to the bathroom and missing recess.

The next day Mr. Lazenby said that because the brown-eyed kids had such a hard time yesterday, blue-eyed kids wouldn't have to do it: he was cancelling the rest of the program. But we did have a discussion. The brown-eyed kids said how awful they'd felt being made to wait around for stuff. Blue-eyeds mostly said brown-eyeds shouldn't have gotten so upset.

* * *

In February it was time for Mike Ierardi's birthday. He lived down the street and had not been mean. Mom suggested I might like to give Mike tickets to "Concert for Peace," with music by Samuel Barber. She said that as part of the present, she would take Mike and me on the city bus to the Rochester Philharmonic, and in the process teach us how to use the bus system. Then we'd be able to go downtown together in the future, on our own, if we wanted.

I liked the concert, and Mike did too, but he wasn't interested in using the bus to go downtown any other time. However, I found out that the same bus ran all the way the other direction as well—toward my school—and that it passed Penfield Town Hall, which had the library in it. I soon got into the habit of skipping the ride home on the school bus, and instead walking the couple of blocks from school to the town library. After two hours, I'd catch the city bus home. I'd get home around six, just before dinner.

I loved being independent: not having to ride the school bus with the mean kids.

After a few months of bus rides from the town library, I decided to try taking the bus the other way—to downtown Rochester, as my mother had first shown me. Mike still wasn't interested, so I'd go by myself.

I settled on early Saturday morning for this first trip, so I'd have all day to look around. I walked to the end of Colonial Village Road and waited until the bus came to take me to Midtown Plaza. Once there, I wasn't sure where to go, but I soon figured out things to do. For instance, there were lots of public telephones—maybe thirty. I checked the coin-return holders on all the phones and found dimes in some. I also looked in the coin returns in all the Coke machines and found coins there too.

That first day I just roamed Midtown Plaza, but over the course of more Saturdays, I found all kinds of amazing places: secret walkways between buildings, access doors to roofs, and good places to buy candy. I was short—four feet, two inches—and I had a special way of darting through the crowds of grown-ups on the sidewalk. I thought of myself as a football running back, getting past tacklers.

That year, I developed a regular route including a store selling hot peanuts, a coin shop with a talking myna bird, several record stores—including my favorite, Jay's Record Mart—and a dozen head shops with names like Leather Soul, Purple Pumpkin and Uhuru. These counterculture stores sold incense, black-light posters, jewelry, clothes, and hash pipes. Their bulletin boards announced rock concerts, such as Woodstock, which I was interested in, but couldn't find any grown-up to take me to.

During the week, I'd save some lunch money; I'd pool this with my two-fifty allowance and on Saturday buy a record. I built up a collection including Blood, Sweat & Tears, The Rolling Stones, The Fifth Dimension, The Who, and Crosby, Stills & Nash. One song on Simon & Garfunkel's *Bridge Over Troubled Waters* album—"The Boxer"—explained how I felt: alone, but refusing to let anyone make me give up my idea of who I was.

* * *

If fourth grade had been hard, fifth grade was worse. The kids who'd been nasty were again in my class, but now they were more threatening. I felt I had no friends around, and I was constantly watching out for fear a gang would beat me up.

But on another level, I felt stronger. During fourth grade I'd discovered that if I paid more attention, I could pass tests and get good grades. In first through third grades I'd gotten B's and C's. In fourth grade I could get A's. By the time I reached fifth grade, it seemed like I could do everything in school fast and well. I had become one of the smartest kids. So, I was bored during class. I was always yelling out answers to questions without waiting to be called on and doing this even while no-one else had a hand up.

Since I knew everyone hated me, and I knew I was smart, I didn't care what the other kids said anymore.

Mrs. Fleming was teaching geometry. "In our world there are three dimensions, length, width and height." She drew a cube on the chalkboard. "We can find out the volume of a cube by multiplying the length times the width times the height."

"Now," she continued, "if you take the surface of a cube, you have a square." She drew a square. "You find the area of the square by multiplying its length times its width. Now, remember the cube is a three-dimensional object: it has length, and width, and height. So, this square is a two-dimensional object since it has length and width but no height."

"Now, if you take the edge of that square, you have a line." She drew a line. "We can find out the length of the line by measuring from point A to point B. The line is a one-dimensional object: it has only length. No width. No height."

"Now, if you just take a point on that line, how many dimensions? Can anybody guess?"

I yelled, "One dimension!"

"No, Andy. Please raise your hand next time. Anyone else?"

No one raised their hand. I raised mine.

"Yes, Andy?"

"Zero dimensions!"

"Yes, Andy, that's right. A point has zero dimensions. Now, because a point has no dimensions, it's very tiny. So tiny it doesn't take up any space. So, since it doesn't take up any space, you can't have two points in the same place. And that's the definition of a point. No two points can be in exactly the same place. Each point has a completely unique place of its own."

I yelled, "Why can't you have two points in the same place?"

"Each point is very, very tiny." She touched her chalk to the blackboard, creating no mark. "It's so small it's completely invisible and takes up no space."

"But that place where you touched the blackboard does take up space."

"Andy, when we draw a point on the blackboard, like this point here, we're not showing the actual point, we're making a picture of the point. The real point is so small that it's just an idea. But it's exactly in its one place. No two points can be in the same place. Points are unique. There's only one of each point. And there are an infinity of points. Everywhere you look, there's a point." She began to poke the air with her finger. "There's a point here, and here, and here. Everywhere, all around you, there are points."

I raised my hand urgently. "Yes, Andy?"

"You could just put another point right on top of the point you picked, and then they'd be in the same place."

A number of other kids started shouting out, "She just said! It's a picture!" and, "Laties, points are invisible!"

I was sitting in one of the front rows. I turned around and looked at another kid. "But if it's so tiny you could just put another point in with it."

Lots of kids were yelling stuff like, "They won't fit!" and "It's invisible!" and "Shut up Laties so we can go to lunch!" Some kids starting gesturing, for my benefit, "Here's a point, here's a point." Soon the whole class was wildly poking fingers in the air, yelling, "Here's a point! Here's a point!"

"Class! Quiet down. Thank you. Andy, would you like to come to the blackboard and show us what you mean?"

I went to the front and picked up the chalk. I ground the chalk into the blackboard. "Here's a point, right?"

Mrs. Fleming said, "All right."

I ground my chalk into exactly the same place, and said, "Here's the other point in the same place!"

The kids all started yelling, "It's on top of the first point! It's not the same!" and "Laties, shut up!"

"Class! Calm down. Andy, the second point is on top of the first point. It's not in the same place. No two points can be in exactly the same place. That's the definition of a point. Each point occupies its very own place and no two points can ever be in the same place."

"But that's not true. I just showed you. Look!" I ground my chalk into the blackboard again.

The kids went wild, poking their fingers in the air, "Here's a point! Here's a point!" and, "Laties! I'm gonna kill you!"

I put the chalk down and went to my seat. I felt excited and nervous. I had discovered something no one knew. I was certain the teacher and kids were wrong. They didn't get it. You could definitely have two points in the same place.

Mrs. Fleming decided I should be allowed to go on independent study. She let me go to a different, empty room while the rest of the class was getting her lectures on math or reading. I was allowed to use the sixth-grade textbooks. As long as I could write out the answers to the questions at the end of each chapter, and pass the tests, I was allowed to push on through these advanced books.

It was great not having to sit through the boring classes. Independent study, all alone, was terrific for me.

I still hung around the town library after school. Since I'd already taken out *Amos Fortune, Free Man* from the school library, on one of my trips to the town library I took out *Black Boy,* by Richard Wright. At the same time, I borrowed a book called *The Way of Zen.* I spent a long time reading *Black Boy.* I had to renew it a couple of times. I identified with this boy people were so mean to.

Then, I borrowed *The Autobiography of Malcolm X.* Mrs. Fleming saw I was carrying it around, and asked, "Why are you reading that?" It took six months, but I did finish. He got killed in the middle of his life. It was the same as with Martin Luther King. Right when he was doing everything.

The Zen book I never figured out, but I carried it with my other books because of just the word, Zen: it seemed secret and different from everything. Later I borrowed this book again, but still couldn't get it.

I signed up for the all-district track meet and practiced for the four-hundred-yard dash by running on our street. The day of the meet, I was sure I'd do well.

Mom drove me. It was at a different school. Fifty kids crowded the starting line. Ready, set, go!

I was in the middle, kicked and bumped. Kids were passing.

I was behind, but there were still kids in back.

It was hard to breathe, and my legs weren't working right.

Everyone was ahead. I could see the finish line. Somebody already won. I realized there was one kid behind, catching up.

Oh! It was John C., the worst bully.

He was panting; his face was red. He looked sideways, and—at the final second—passed me.

I came in last.

Luckily, I didn't care.

My one good friend was Tom Weiss: we'd played together since we were babies. Our dads were colleagues—University of Rochester professors who studied the effects of pollution on behavior. Dad and Bernie Weiss trained pigeons and rats to peck buttons and run mazes, then dosed the animals with carbon monoxide, methyl mercury, dioxin or PCBs, and measured how this changed their actions. They served on National Institutes of Health panels, advising the government on industrial pollution limits. They favored stricter controls than other scientists, since the effects they thought important were behavioral—like tremors or hyperactivity—while other policy advisors thought you had to see cancer before a pollution level was too high.

Dad told me it would one day be proven that learning problems and violent actions of urban youth were because of exposure to lead in the paint and plumbing of inner-city housing.

Our dads' laboratory was in Strong Memorial Hospital. Tom and I loved running around the hospital's back corridors and stairways. Every Saturday night, I'd sleep at Tom's house or he'd sleep at mine. We'd stay up till one AM, watching horror movies on TV, then sneak out and roam in the woods, or over in Mount Hope Cemetery.

Also, at Tom's house, there was a reel-to-reel recorder; we'd make long tapes of ourselves as if we were a late-night radio show.

When we were twelve, we went by ourselves to a Frank Zappa concert, at the War Memorial arena. The air was thick with weed smoke. John McLaughlin and the Mahavishnu Orchestra were the opening act. McLaughlin and Zappa both played lots of super-fast guitar solos, and Frank Zappa's songs were crazy: Go to Montana and grow dental floss; don't eat yellow snow.

THE MUSIC THIEF

* * *

Dad loved bookstores. My two sisters and I took for granted lots of bookstore visits and our houseful of books. At age ten, I helped my sister Nancy organize my parents' collection. We put poetry at the top of the stairs, history at the bottom, fine art in the bathroom, fiction in the basement. We counted three thousand books. Browsing my parents' books was an introduction to world culture, science, and the arts.

On Sundays and holidays, outings to bookstores topped the agenda. Dad's rule was that, if you entered a bookstore and stayed for fifteen minutes, you had to support that store by buying a book, so at every store, we kids were allowed to choose books for ourselves. I came to specialize in mythology, archaeology, European literature, and poetry. My bedroom filled up with books I'd picked.

At age fifteen, on a solo bus ride, I reviewed my childhood visits to bookstores and was able to visualize five hundred.

I'd been scared of drowning since I was eight, when water got in my snorkel. At fifteen, I still hadn't learned to swim. The gym teacher made me stay in the shallow end of the pool, while he gave lessons in the deep end. Every Tuesday and Thursday, five rough kids would surround me and hold my head under water; the gym teacher refused to intervene and wouldn't let me sit out the class.

Monday and Wednesday nights, I couldn't sleep. I thought of the quote Mom had told me when I was little,

"The coward dies a thousand deaths, the brave man dies but once." I couldn't get out of my head the nagging question, "But what about that once?"

One day, during my half hour of torture, I found myself shouting, *"Cogito, ergo sum! Cogito, ergo sum!"*

"Shut up, Laties. What are you saying anyway?"

"I think, therefore I am."

"Why don't you just talk English?"

"Cogito, ergo sum! Cogito, ergo sum!"

"Laties, you're weird." Then they forced my head under.

After several weeks of this, I finally refused to get in the pool. The gym teacher threatened me with suspension, and I said I didn't care; I'd learn to swim on my own.

I signed up for lessons at Perkins Swim Club. The following week, I stood in the shallow end of their pool, towering over fifteen splashing five-year-old beginners. The pretty girl who taught our group found me amusing. At least I'd shot up to five-nine. I did learn to swim.

Dad had a huge big-band jazz collection; his records were always playing. As a kid in Boston, he'd seen Duke Ellington and Count Basie live on stage at a fancy movie house—they'd played between double-feature films. Dad encouraged me to take instrument lessons. He suggested flute, because it was light to carry. I started the summer after the concert for Martin Luther King.

But—I really wanted to learn saxophone. I switched a year later. It was way heavier—but way louder, which I liked.

I was ten years old on the stage of the Penfield High School auditorium, ready to stumble through the third-saxophone part in an all-district elementary school band concert, when a tall, bright-eyed guy with a funny little beard squatted down in front of me, put his face up to mine, and said, "A saxophone player! I'll be waiting for you in the high school jazz band!"

That was '70, but by '73, when I'd arrived in ninth grade, I'd already quit band out of boredom with the regular concert music, and high-school music teacher Ned Corman—that guy with the funny beard—had been demoted by the superintendent to a middle-school job for refusing to stop running his jazz band, and instead start a football marching band.

I wasn't concerned at Ned's absence. For me, music was no longer a school thing. I played flute and harmonica in my bedroom for pleasure, and joined my friend Bill Meade's Friday jams, playing my sax as loudly as possible while bass and drums thumped Eric Clapton's tune, "Sunshine of Your Love."

But other kids were wearing t-shirts around school that said, "Give Us This Day Our Daily Ned." And by eleventh grade, Ned was back. He'd taken the district to the New York Supreme Court and won what came to be recognized as a landmark victory. On his unpaid time, he could run jazz bands and not marching bands, if that was what he decided.

In October of '75, I was walking home along Penfield Road when a car swerved onto the shoulder ahead. The window rolled down. Ned Corman poked out his head and shouted, "Andy!"

I didn't know he knew my name. I was only dimly aware of who he was. My school identity was well established. I was the school paper's news editor. I was on the chess team.

"Andy!"

On the other hand, I did remember him from that moment before the fifth-grade all-district concert. I didn't feel like I was even connected to that little kid, but I did know Ned was the guy who'd talked as if high school was tomorrow.

I walked slowly toward his car. He was leaning way out the window, the upper part of his body twisted backward, calling enthusiastically over the noise of the passing cars, "Andy! I want to see you in jazz band, Tuesday after school!"

"I don't have time."

He was insistent, and after all he was a celebrity, because he'd bucked the school administration. Plus, I was flattered he remembered me from fifth grade. So, I gave in and said okay.

I showed up at jazz band, and we rehearsed the charts. When it was time for someone to improvise, I listened. After a few tunes, Ned called on me. I didn't know what to play. Certainly, it shouldn't be wild the way I was with Bill Meade. Bass, drums and piano were going; I fielded a couple of notes, the solo was past, and I was relieved. On the next tune, some other student did the same thing: when called, they played a few notes, then luckily solo time was done. I think we all felt the same: worried about sounding off-key, but aware it wouldn't last long. Getting called to solo was like getting a shot at the doctor. After you were finished, you felt like you'd gotten past danger, so the relief was the reward. And people would whisper, "Sounded good!" Even though I was pretty sure it hadn't, that felt nice, and I'd say the same to them when they'd done their solo: "Fantastic!" I liked being the one telling someone they'd done great. Being their appreciative listener. Gradually, we all got more comfortable with how we sounded together.

Ned didn't teach us to solo. He didn't say we had to stick to such-and-such a scale, or such-and-such notes. He'd just yell, "Andy!" And I got more confident that my noisy, intuitive approach was okay—because no matter what I played, he'd visibly—wiggling his hips as he pushed the rhythm forward—really, be enjoying my music.

There was just one piece of advice I heard Ned offer many times: "If you're gonna make a mistake, make it loud!"

Penfield High School had its politicized atmosphere because its district straddled two different suburbs. Penfield was more Republican and Christian; Brighton was more Democratic and Jewish. Economically there were a number of fault lines: there were some kids who lived in nice houses like mine; others lived in the trailer park. It wasn't an easy school to run, and the administration had their hands full with drug use and vandalism.

The principal decided too many kids were in the hallways while classes were in session, and announced a policy requiring any student to have a signed pass permitting them to move between rooms. A bunch of my friends circulated a flyer titled *Screw the Pass,* featuring a picture of a screw (the kind you use with a screwdriver) going through a kid's head. There were two paragraphs of complaints about the policy.

Screw the Pass had been written and printed by members of the track team: Brian Cooper, Paul Gulino, Bill Heinrich (my friend Phil's big brother), and Bill Meade. The principal didn't know this, but he did suspend Brian—one of the school's few Black students—on the basis of having been caught passing out the flyer.

I wasn't involved. I was already the news editor of *Upper Story*—the regular school newspaper—and writing about the stupid rules. But the night of Brian Cooper's suspension, a bunch of us got t-shirts made that said, on the front: "Free Brian Cooper," and on the back "Screw the Pass." I wore mine all day. None of my teachers asked me to cover it up—which I took to be a sign of sympathy.

The vice principal pulled me out of chemistry class and when I refused to put on a sweater over the t-shirt, he brought me down to the principal's office.

The principal had concluded that I was the one behind the whole flyer thing. He accused me directly, and when I said I hadn't known it was going to happen, but I agreed with the flyer, he said I must know who had done it—and I said I did. He said this proved I was responsible.

I stated, "Just because I know an elephant has big ears, doesn't mean I put the big ears on the elephant."

The principal leapt to his feet, slammed his palm on his desk, and shouted, "Suspended! He's suspended! Call his mother!"

They called Mom, who agreed to come pick me up. This was unnecessary, since for the past few years, I'd been walking the three miles from school every day.

Mom drove me home, and said, "A man's reach should exceed his grasp, or what's a heaven for?" Her support was great.

The track-team journalists maintained secrecy, even as they enlisted more authors, and pumped out frequent underground newspapers. The administration was going nuts. Meanwhile, since I'd been suspended, I became a revolutionary celebrity. Even the kids who'd been harassing me since fourth grade about my long hair—since ninth, I'd worn it in a ponytail—started encouraging me to keep fighting with the principal. A few months later, I ran for student representative to the school board, and won.

The ringleaders graduated, so a bunch of us—including jazz-band trombonist Mitch Ahern, student-council president Mike Ierardi, and former *Upper Story* editor Laura Kelsey—figured we'd better take up the slack. While the first year, the underground paper had been called *FightBack,* we decided to strike a more positive note. We called it *FightForward.*

    I was also on the school board, and I sat on the dais with the adult board members. I was allowed to talk during the meetings. Some of the members clearly didn't like me, but some were sympathetic: two of my fellow jazz-band members' mothers were on the board—Ruth Phillips and Robin Baxendall. (Ned Corman had urged them to join.)

    It was from Robin that I found out the superintendent was slandering me in executive session. Robin called and asked, did I have a master key to the school, and was I going in at night? I certainly did not have a master key. I hung around whenever I wanted, though: several custodians were my friends. But I didn't want to be there except to play jazz, and go to student council meetings, and do theater, and play chess—well, yes, I was there a lot. More than the administration liked.

I seemed to be making those guys nervous. I'd developed a relationship with the Rochester branch of the American Civil Liberties Union. Also, Mom had taught me how to do research downtown, in a law library.

I'd used the ACLU once already. For a few years I'd quietly skipped the "under God" phrase in the pledge of allegiance, and then in eleventh grade I'd decided America was not the home of liberty and justice for all, so I'd started refusing to say the pledge entirely. My homeroom teacher had complained to the principal about my not standing up, and my silence. When the principal had threatened to discipline me, I'd spoken with the ACLU, and director Loren Warboys had sent a letter to the high school that laid out my right to remain silent during the pledge.

I'd agreed with the vice principal on a compromise: I would wait outside the homeroom door each morning until the other students had said the pledge, then I'd enter and take my seat for the attendance taking.

Especially after this experience, I was confident in exercising my constitutionally-protected civil liberties in school.

FightForward had three themes: administration bullying, student apathy, and freedom of speech. Because the principal was trying to make us submit to his editing, before we distributed, and because I didn't conceal that this year I was part of the project, it was a more straightforward fight for him than it had been the year before, when he hadn't known he was fighting the track team.

Our secret weapon was our parents' aid: especially Mitch Ahern's access to his father's high-speed Ektaprint 225 copy machine—then in development at Kodak Corporation—which enabled us to produce two-thousand copies of the six-page paper, six times during the 76/77 school year, at no expense.

People would ask, "Are you really gonna sue the principal?" If he punished us severely, we were. The Supreme Court ruled against our side fifteen years later, but at the time, the law was with us. School administrators weren't allowed to enforce rules that said students had to submit newspapers for review before distribution. Also, the principal was allowed to punish us after we'd distributed only if what we'd said was libel, that is, actual lies. The ACLU was ready to sue, and our paper often focused on what the administration had done during the previous distribution. It made great copy.

Distributing was so much fun. The teachers had been told that if they saw any sign that one of our papers was being distributed, they should seize the copies and tell the main office, so additional teachers could be told to intervene. We'd have ten students enter the school by different entrances, each carrying two-hundred copies of *FightForward*. These ten had each lined up ten friends to whom they'd pass off twenty papers. These hundred would run around and give away twos and fives and tell people to pass them on. Naturally, when distribution was in progress, kids were grabbed by teachers, but it was usually with a small number of papers. The administration never succeeded in preventing a full-school distribution—it only took twenty minutes.

FightForward was read much more avidly than the official *Upper Story* paper.

The hubbub in Penfield caused the *Rochester Times-Union* to write an article about us, in which the vice principal was quoted referring to *FightForward's* editors as a group of "so-called pseudo-intellectuals." We loved that.

In May, our writer Matt Perry handed me a lengthy, inflammatory, and profound piece for the graduation issue of *FightForward.* We published "The Right to Your Rights" unedited.

It started off with a bang:

"Where are you going without a pass?"

"You can't go out there. Come in here. You're not supervised."

"Where were you yesterday? You weren't on the absentee bulletin."

"Where are your white socks?"

FUCK YOU.

Fuck you a hundred times and stick it up your ass sideways. That's what you would like to say to the people who ask you that type of question, especially if it is one of The Big Three Buffoons. But instead you say some bullshitty thing and walk away with your palms still sweating cause Christ almighty you almost got in trouble for doing something you weren't supposed to do....

Then, Matt transitioned to a psychology of ethics:

Being punished by your parents when you were young, and even now, is a method of imposing what they think is right or wrong on your mind. This is how you come to develop a moral code, what you think is right and what is wrong. When you punish someone for doing something wrong, you're attempting to take part of his mind and make it think the way you do....
    What is right and what is wrong is relative. What I think is right might not be what you think is right....
    Think about it. Is walking down the hall of a building so wrong? Is going outside of the building and sitting in the shade so bad? Is cutting class such a sin that the kid must be removed from school, abridging his right to learn? Is preventing a child from graduating high school because he did not complete a certain number of gym classes justified?...

Matt concluded with a rousing call for individual transformation:

Don't feel guilty about such silly things as leaving the school illegally, not using hall passes and wearing something other than those goddamn white socks. When you get rid of your guilt feelings about these and other trivial rules then you will have made the first step out of this wretched mess called Penfield High School.

For the year's final school board meeting, a vote was scheduled on whether to end the prior review rule for student publications. Most of the board members had told me they planned to vote yes, as a sort of present to me for having done a good job as student representative.

But Matt's article—in the issue of *FightForward* we'd distributed the day before the meeting—infuriated the board members. Several made speeches saying they now agreed with the principal that students couldn't be trusted to show good judgment in their publishing decisions. I answered that if the content of one offensive—but in no way libelous—article could interfere with the board's resolve to abide by the United States Constitution's First Amendment free speech guarantee, then a board vote to lift the prior review rule would have been meaningless in any case. They'd probably have reinstated the rule in the fall.

After the meeting, board member Clint Hutto cut loose at me, demanding how I could show such disrespect for the principal. I said, "I didn't write that article, but I support the author's right to express his opinion. Supreme Court Justice Oliver Wendell Holmes said, 'We should be eternally vigilant against attempts to check the expression of opinions that we loathe.'"

Hutto snorted and walked away.

A week later, the students elected Matt Perry to be their next student representative to the school board.

2-IN AND OUT AT YALE

SEPTEMBER 1977

Starting at Yale was different for me than for most other freshmen. My sister Nancy provided a ready-made group of friends. One of her roommates, Kate Sanderson, was a terrific jazz pianist, and we formed a band with Jahmes Finlayson on percussion, and Greg Jarby on bass. I also jammed frequently with Ted Sabety, who played a ferocious electric guitar: he was studying jazz-rock/fusion with Larry Coryell. One afternoon we drove out country roads to Ted's friend the drummer's house and had the loudest jam ever. When you play sax loud, it's pretty loud. Drums are louder than saxophones. But Ted and our friend Phil—a violinist who had an electric pick-up—could turn up their amps as much as they wanted. A mere unelectrified sax was pretty much drowned. I probably suffered some hearing loss.

My jazz-band friend Brad Phillips had once compared my raucous improvising to John Coltrane. I bought my first Coltrane album shortly after getting this compliment and fell in love. By the time I arrived at Yale a year later, I was a jazz-record addict. One of the first albums I bought in New Haven was *The George Lewis Solo Trombone Record,* just released. George Lewis was an astonishing virtuoso from the Association for the Advancement of Creative Musicians, in Chicago. He was also a Yalie, who'd graduated a few years before. My favorite track was "Toneburst—Piece For 3 Trombones Simultaneously"—a triumph of innovative overdubbing—although, his heartbreaking rendition of the Billy Strayhorn standard "Lush Life" was also a tour de force.

    I started buying more and more AACM records: Art Ensemble of Chicago, Anthony Braxton, Roscoe Mitchell. The dozens of AACM musicians combined over-the-top improvisational prowess with shockingly weird but highly disciplined compositional structures. What they referred to as "creative music" was passionate and totally unpredictable.

Coed dorms!

    Sitting on the floor of my room, Maya Lin and I compared families: we'd each run cup-and-string telephones to our older sibling's bedroom (her, brother; me, sister).

    She puzzled over our generation's disengagement: we were the end of the baby boom, the sheltered ones. The older boomers had fought in or protested the Vietnam War; the war hadn't reached us—we'd been home.

    I agreed this was certainly true of most kids. I didn't tell her about my years of long-haired protest. After the US had left Vietnam in '75, I'd cut my hair short to play Dr. Bradman in *Blithe Spirit*. Bragging about being bullied would be weird.

    She was so self-possessed. Dazzled by her super-long, black hair, I couldn't figure out how to make a move.

    Life was complicated enough: in my first month, already two women had kissed me.

THE MUSIC THIEF

* * *

I had a long talk with my roommate Kane St. John, who was planning to major in history. He sketched out his life—graduate school and a university career—then said, "So—I guess that's it? Fifty years as a history professor, then retirement?"

Dad was a toxicology professor. Uncle Alan was an ophthalmology professor. Uncle George was a plant physiology professor. My childhood had been spent among graduate students—aged ten, I was the bartender at department holiday parties—and I'd had this same conversation with Dad about how I saw my life unfolding: first graduate school in archaeology, then a university career, with summers excavating in Egypt or Mexico.

But within a week of arriving at Yale, I'd seen a brightly-painted audition board advertising try-outs for *James and the Giant Peach*. I'd done lots of theater in high school. I'd read *James* as a kid and decided to audition. The director, Kerro Knox, cast me as Old Green Grasshopper.

The Yale Dramat Children's Theater Company had been founded the year before by Kerro, Kay Saakvitne, Rhonda Lipkin, Todd Bethel and several others. We staged three rambunctious shows during my freshman year and toured them into schools in the surrounding suburbs: Branford, Fairfield, and East Haven. I played Humbug in *The Phantom Tollbooth*, and the newspaper boy in Rich Selden's *The Daily Newsical Musical*. The kids loved our disruptive invasions of their tightly-regulated schools, and I loved being the disrupter.

* * *

I took only one archaeology course and it was boring. Maybe the previous summer's physical work of excavating at Bordesley Abbey, outside Birmingham, England, had spoiled me. I wasn't interested in the speculation and the theory. And somehow, I knew my professor didn't want to be teaching in a lecture hall—he'd rather have been doing fieldwork.

I took spoken Egyptian Arabic all year, and excitedly applied to go to Egypt, to excavate during the summer. But—this time I was rejected, because I hadn't learned to read hieroglyphs.

The rejection caught me off guard. I'd been through an incredible run of success. Everything I'd applied for, I'd gotten. I'd been living a dream.

Confused, I went back through the Archaeological Association of America's '78 fieldwork bulletin and found I'd missed deadlines for lots of other summer excavations. I ended up applying to work in rural Delaware, looking at patterns of Native American migration a thousand years ago.

There were five of us living together at the Island Field Museum, outside of Milford, Delaware. It was a sort of airplane hangar sheltering a Native American graveyard. You could walk on an elevated platform around the graves. Each had been meticulously opened; the skeletons were exposed, in their original curled up positions.

They looked cold.

I lived there six weeks. We didn't spend much time in the graveyard—we lived in the building attached. We'd go out each morning and systematically walk in fields and forests, staring at the ground, looking for flint flakes from toolmaking, or shards of pottery. If we found clusters of these, we'd dig a trial pit—three feet wide by three feet long. We'd go down in ten-inch levels, tossing dirt into a tray with a screened bottom; this swung from a trestle. Anything that turned up in the sifting, like potsherds or burnt stones, would be kept in a bag, labeled by its level.

In this way, we collected evidence documenting the seasonal movement of ancient tribes from the Delmarva peninsula to the Appalachian foothills.

I spent weekends playing street music in New York City.

Every Friday at four, my co-worker Kerry would go home to Staten Island, to spend the weekend with his girlfriend; he'd give me a lift as far as the Staten Island Ferry. My routine was to catch the eight o'clock ferry to Manhattan, position myself right in front—either upstairs or down—get out my saxophone, and improvise. I stuck to standards: I played Gershwin's "Summertime" a lot because people seemed to like it, but I also had Duke Ellington tunes like "Take the A Train," and "Mood Indigo."

There was usually another musician or band on the ferry. Sometimes, while I was tootling on the lower deck, a three-piece klezmer group wailed on the upper deck. Another regular was a folksinger with guitar. When we reached Manhattan, I'd take the train to the World Trade Center, ride to the observation deck, and relax, gazing down at the city. I'd continue uptown, to spend the night at Bill Meade's apartment on the Upper West Side; he was enrolled at Manhattan School of Music.

I'd continue playing street music Saturday and Sunday. I met the most amazing people. In front of Macy's, a blind man with a tin cup approached, shouting, "My place, nine years! My place, nine years!" I refused to leave, and he settled a little way over, rattling his change.

Playing in front of the Village Gate, Raphael D'Lugoff—the son of the owner—invited me onto the stage Dizzy Gillespie would be playing that night. We jammed on "Blue Monk."

Another time in the Village, some cops rushed up and yelled they'd told me to move along yesterday, and what was I doing back again? When I protested that I hadn't been here yesterday, they grabbed my sax and said if I didn't leave, they'd "impound the horn."

In Penn Station, I met a guy who told stories of street people. A lady he knew had ninety-thousand dollars in the bank, but wouldn't go back to her house, because her son would put her in a nursing home.

In front of the Broadway musical *Bubbling Brown Sugar*, I was doing well while the show was going, but before intermission a magician showed up and told me it was his territory. His name was Mad Max. I got out of the way as he seemed professional. After his performance, I asked how he dealt with hecklers. He demonstrated how he'd scare them with the threat he was going to curse them, getting a crazy look in his eyes, his hands trembling wildly.

When I was playing in front of the lions at the New York Public Library, a drunk guy danced for a while, and finally, in a mushy voice, asked if I knew "Melancholy Baby." I fumbled through.

Fifteen years later, I'd arrived at Chicago Public Radio's studio to do a show about children's books, when legendary jazz pianist Marian McPartland emerged from the interview booth, where she'd been talking about the interesting history of the tune "Melancholy Baby." I told her I'd been a street musician in New York in '78 and played "Melancholy Baby" as a request from a drunk. She said, "I didn't know street musicians took requests."

That was the only request I ever got. The status of street musicians in the US is depressingly low. In Europe, people appreciate us, but here we're thought of as beggars.

Bill Meade took me to have my palm read by the security guard at Manhattan School of Music.

"You are a young soul—you came from Pluto nine-hundred years ago…. You were a German woman in the nineteenth century…. You will live to be eighty-one. What career are you planning?"

"I'm trying to decide between archaeology and music."

He was still looking at my hand. "You will have chosen which path by age twenty-nine."

As we walked away, Bill said, "I'm an old soul—came from Jupiter twelve-thousand years ago."

He always had me beat.

After my stint in Delaware I took a semester off Yale and kept excavating. I'd been hired as an experienced volunteer, by Trent Valley Archaeological Research Committee, in Nottingham, England—my first and last paid archaeological position, featuring free room and fifteen-pound-a-week stipend.

There was a lot of archaeology in England because the government paid for it. This project, the excavation of Nottingham Castle, was county funded. The premise was enhancement of a tourist attraction. The need was clear: Nottingham Castle—the site of Robin Hood's travails—wasn't there. Where it had stood, there was now a large manor house: the castle had been demolished in the sixteen-hundreds. That made a lot to dig.

I was assigned to work, along with a caving expert, in a well choked with rocks. Denny would attach a rope to a harness around my waist, then use a pully system to lower me forty feet. At the bottom of the well, I'd secure a second rope around a huge rock, and, while Denny was pulling up my rope and the rock's, I'd clamber up the indentations in the well-shaft's sides, sticking out a hand to keep the rising rock from spinning.

Later, we spent weeks digging out a gigantic hedge—piling dirt into a wheelbarrow, rolling it down a driveway, around a corner, up a steep plank to the top of a dumpster and, with a burst of energy, flipping the barrow and dumping the dirt.

One of the guys on this excavation, George, was a fan of trad jazz—that is, New Orleans music—Dixieland—which was popular in England. On weekends, we went to trad pubs together, and George encouraged me to jam with the musicians. I knew the basics of Dixieland theory but had zero experience playing it. These English musicians were tolerant though, and I didn't sit in for more than one tune any night.

The English trad players were true to the classic form. They knew twenties jazz inside out, clearly having learned their craft playing with the records, memorizing licks and turnarounds note for note, the universally-acknowledged way to imbibe the styles of the jazz masters. This approach requires a high degree of discipline and excellent listening skills.

In some odd sense, too, the trad players seemed to identify emotionally with their imaginary versions of the original musicians. One night, in a packed pub, an excellent Louis-Armstrong-style trumpet player picked up a mic and, in a husky Armstrong-baritone, launched into "What Did I Do to Be So Black and Blue?" This 1929 song refers to race violence in America: white people beating up Black people until they're black and blue. You never hear it these days because it's racist. It takes the perspective of a subservient Black man who pleads he hasn't done anything to deserve a beating. The song is not an attack on white people who beat Black people. It's just an expression of sadness in the face of the inevitable way things are. Singing songs like this into the forties and fifties caused Louis Armstrong to lose his credibility with leading jazz musicians of those decades. Miles Davis was intensely critical of Armstrong for pandering to white audiences—even though Davis did follow in Armstrong's tradition of careful, spare note-selection.

I knew the Armstrong version of "Black and Blue." Watching this tall, strong-jawed white Englishman reproduce every inflection of Armstrong's weird lament somehow translated the whole English trad experience for me. These musicians felt that American white culture was too ignorant to understand the brilliance of American Black musicians, but English musicians and their audiences did understand and celebrate this marvelous music, even to the extent of identifying with its oppressed creators. So, singing "Black and Blue" was all right because the white singer specifically wasn't a white American, and therefore he was qualified to indict white Americans for their brand of racism.

Simultaneously, he conveyed to his audience the nice, safe kinds of Black people whose work he was purveying.

Overlaying everything was the jokey, we-should-never-have-let-the-colonies-go-because-look-what-those-idiots-did-next stuff some English people lay on Americans.

Weekday evenings I practiced sax in my room and read. I immersed myself in Seamus Heaney's *Death of a Naturalist*. I studied *The Selected Poems of Laura Riding*. Her "Autobiography of the Present" began:

> Whole is by breaking and by mending.
> The body is a day of ruin,
> The mind, a moment of repair.
> A day is not a day of mind
> Until all lifetime is repaired despair.

Most of all, I loved Ursula K. Le Guin's *The Dispossessed,* which I'd found at Mushroom Bookshop, a radical bookstore. A guy in the grip of the beauty of knowledge discovers a universal principle of physics—simultaneity—and safeguards the autonomy of his planet's anarchist society. Such a character is not often to be encountered in literature.

I became a frequent customer at Mushroom. I grasped the root meaning of the key anarchist phrase, "property is theft"—as the historical Robin Hood and his freely associating troupe of merry men surely did, but which has been glossed over in their legend.

I did understand the implausibility of anarchism as a social system for our existing culture. My reading that fall confirmed that the leading theorists had their doubts as well. Herbert Read the English art critic said in *Anarchy and Order* that at a fancy dinner party a well-known lady asked his politics. He answered, "I am an anarchist," and she replied, "How absurd!" Read wrote that on reflection, he'd decided she was right.

I agreed. Anarchism was absurd because there was no way everyone could be forced to act altruistically. So, a society of mutual aid, direct action, decentralization, and no private property couldn't be made to come into being.

Because this seemed obvious, I couldn't understand the advocacy by a branch of the movement for violence as a route to the anarchist society.

Direct action—making your actions in life co-ordinate with your values and aspirations for the freedom of others—felt sensible to me. But I didn't think the ends justified the means. If you used violence, you wouldn't achieve a nonviolent society.

I felt that anarchists should set a good example, to induce a nonviolent society to emerge. They could do this by refusing to fall back on the absurd lives they'd been handed at birth: they should exercise their freedom to choose what lives they'd lead. Anyone could choose altruism.

True, in the context of our cut-throat culture, such an existential decision would also be absurd.

So, reading Ursula K. Le Guin clarified my thinking. I realized I was searching for a compassionate approach to creating my life. And, that any social action in which I engaged should emerge from personal growth, not be directed against anyone. All of which hearkened back to the Beatles song about self-transformation that I'd liked as a ten-year-old, "Revolution."

It was settled, by mail, that when I returned next semester, I'd become producer for the children's theater, since Rhonda Lipkin didn't have time to keep doing it, and no one else was willing.

I left Nottingham in mid-December and spent a week in New Haven. Rhonda clued me into a slew of new programs, breakthroughs, and issues. We'd launched weekly drama workshops at two public-housing projects: Quinnapiac Valley and Dixwell Homes. We were offering theater classes at Lee High School. We'd broken into the New Haven public elementary schools. There'd been a dust-up with JD Salinger. We'd produced *Catcher in the Rye,* and while it was touring, Salinger's girlfriend had found out. Salinger had threatened to sue us and the dean had insisted we cancel the tour.

Rhonda had already booked the performance venues for *Hunting of the Snark*, which Kerro Knox would be directing. She gave me notebooks full of information and said I could ask her questions as the season progressed.

Yale Dramat Children's Theater Company had no faculty advisor, and no formal Yale affiliation. Although its name suggested it was a creature of the Dramat—the undergraduate theater organization—in fact, people there paid no attention to us. We used their facilities to build sets, props, and costumes, and we had a little office next to their green room. Otherwise we were a loose assortment of interested students, most of whom were also involved with regular Dramat productions now and then.

Since there was an idea floating around that it would be fun for a bunch of us to stay in New Haven next summer and run our program full time, I decided to try pull this together during my spring run as producer, aiming to convene an anarchist collective, with actors sharing all responsibilities.

Bridging the town/gown divide was an important goal for us, so we decided we'd also open the summer company to actors who lived in New Haven but had no Yale connection. We advertised auditions in the *New Haven Register,* and to our shock, fifty people showed up for tryouts.

We broke the group into threes and fours, handed out poems and short stories, and gave the teams forty-five minutes to whip together sketches. Everyone watched each other's performances. The work was fabulous. There were thirty strong actors in the group. A few of us regulars narrowed the list down and made clear what kind of money we'd be offering, which was—we had no idea. But it was early. There was time to come up with stipends.

I wrote grant proposals to local corporations and met with representatives of foundations. None were impressed with our theater—or me. We'd existed three years. We had no advisor or legal status. We had no theater space of our own. I was nineteen.

Julia Poirier was playing the beaver in *Hunting of the Snark*. She suggested I contact Dwight Hall, the locus for a number of Yale/New Haven collaborations. This was our breakthrough. Dwight Hall offered twenty-five-hundred dollars from the Yale Charities Drive for actor stipends, and we were then able to persuade several other funders to ante up smaller amounts. The biology department offered us the use of a van, and the department of maintenance said they'd pay for gas. Fenno Heath, the Yale Glee Club Director—another of Julia Poirier's friends—said we could use his space at Hendrie Hall to raise money with public performances.

The body of our schedule was free shows, which we booked into New Haven summer schools, Boys and Girls Clubs, park-district programs, and YMCA day camps. I also arranged for us to extend the Quinnapiac Valley and Dixwell Homes drama workshops, increasing the frequency to twice a week, and I added the Fairhaven Neighborhood Corporation day camp and the West Rock Neighborhood Corporation day camp.

We maintained our Lee High School classes through June, touring *Horton Hatches the Egg* into nearby elementary schools. The young children had a great time watching their big brothers and sisters acting out this Dr. Seuss book, back in their own former schools.

As the summer approached, we found housing sublets to share; we rented four apartments among us. We divided costume-building, set-creation, directing, workshop-presenting, and show-booking as evenly as we could. This didn't work out fairly, and friction emerged as the summer played out, since some actors were doing more than others. I was incapable of resolving these issues; luckily the season wasn't long enough for the tension to get too bad.

We produced six shows to tour in repertory. Kerro Knox directed *Alice in Wonderland;* I was the White Rabbit. Kerro also staged *Aesop's Fables,* for which I played Aesop. In *There Ain't No Bugs on Me*—American folktales selected and directed by our English member, Rachel Feldberg—I played Saint Peter. In Rich Selden's *Fred, a Stair,* I was the next-to-last stair leading to the roof. I adapted and directed Italo Calvino's *The Distance of the Moon.* We cancelled the tour for Debbie Taylor and Barbara Chusid's musical adaptation of *The Great Quillow* upon receiving a confused letter from James Thurber's ninety-year-old widow, rejecting our rights request.

Touring free performances exclusively, which had been our plan, wouldn't support our actors, so we decided to also earn money, touring to sites that could pay fees. We booked ourselves into summer camps, waterfront resorts, and even nursing homes. These extra shows taxed us: we worked nonstop, in six weeks producing a hundred events.

On a given morning we'd fan out to run drama workshops, then by eleven AM, regroup to present *Alice in Wonderland* at a fancy summer camp like Choate-Rosemary Hall. By afternoon, we'd be performing *Aesop* at a Boys Club. At night we'd rehearse our upcoming play. The Saturday performances on campus were each show's well-attended culmination.

My effort to attract support from Baker Salsbury, director of the New Haven Arts Council, continued all summer. Baker gamely attended two performances. Both times, we were having trouble with the venue's promoter and their sound system, so the work wasn't up to snuff. At a follow-up meeting in his office, he told me frankly that he didn't think we were good.

"You saw problem shows. At schools, the teachers say they love us."

"You listen to what teachers say? What do they know about theater? Audience members are the last people you should be paying attention to."

"Then why should I listen to you?"

"Andy, I spent many years performing in regional theater. I was assistant dean at Yale School of Drama. When you ask an audience member if they liked your show, of course they'll say yes. They're being polite. You can't give credence to that any more than to a critic who gives you a bad review. Only you can decide for yourself if you're doing quality work. But if you're going to listen to an outsider, it has to be a professional who can evaluate you objectively. And I'm telling you, your performances are rough. When the

New Haven Arts Council funds a group, that's a seal of approval, and you're not ready."

A few days later, I complained about Baker's criticisms to a student officer of the Yale Dramat, who replied, "You know what they say at the drama school about him: Baker Salsbury doesn't talk, he farts."

Nobody said theater people are tactful.

Yes, some things went wrong. People got mad, and we got mad back. Mix-ups led to missed opportunities. But we did what we said, reaching thousands of New Haven kids with free shows and workshops.

And we had fun. We'd show up at a housing project we'd never been to, pile out of the van and put on half an hour of *Aesop,* to the shock and pleasure of the kids, and the alarm and amusement of their parents. Then we'd drive to the East Haven beach and launch into American folk songs from *There Ain't No Bugs on Me,* right there on the sand, in the midst of families sunning and swimming. The summer children's theater was so popular that actor Ann Klotz was able to carry it off as producer the following two years, then hand it on to another producer. The program became a staple of Yale/New Haven life for twenty years.

Despite my promising start on the road to becoming a professor of archaeology, in May I'd informed the dean I was dropping out. It was as a former student that I worked with the summer children's theater.

Shuttling between drama workshops with desperately poor kids at the Quinnapiac Valley Housing Project and fun late-night jam sessions on the rich Yale campus, I'd started to get irritated with myself. I knew perfectly well that despite all my labels—archaeological fieldworker, children's-theater producer, jazz musician—I was really just an American middle-class kid taking advantage of the special opportunities the accident of birth had conferred.

My decision was triggered by the theft of my sax. I'd left it in the children's-theater office and locked the door. But the window had been unlocked. The cop said, "You lost a lot." Yes, but it was Ned Corman who'd selected—and Dad who'd paid for—that great alto sax. I walked over to Goldie & Libro and bought myself a used soprano sax, wondering who'd next be playing my alto. Horns do change hands.

I couldn't stop thinking about the perspective of the thief. I had a key to Yale. He came in through the window.

Property is theft.

I didn't feel something as dumb as guilt. More lack of creativity. I was living in a dream world. I came up with an image of my Yale life as a luscious red apple: not ripe, dyed. Nothing I'd done had earned me what I had. Everything had fallen in my lap. No matter how much effort I put out, on no matter how many fronts, I was still just a representative of my ideal, white, two-parent suburban childhood.

Even worse, I knew this set of feelings was a cliché among guys like me. I knew the tune "The Middle Class," from *Jacques Brel is Alive and Well and Living in Paris,* in which three young men denounce their parents' generation only to discover, at the end of the song, that they've turned into the stodgy older generation being jeered by new upstarts. Like my freshman roommate Kane, I could foresee my life, so of course, I understood the silliness of acting the rebel. At some point, my tantrum would subside, and there I'd be, living like my parents, in the burbs.

But. Even in light of this knowledge, I decided to try to create a different life for myself. Not as an act of defiance against my family or my social class—though this was a spice I couldn't dismiss—but, rather as an aesthetic, even existential decision.

Because it seemed like—at some level—that whole Andy-Laties-the-archaeology-professor life had already happened, since I knew it would, if I stuck with the program.

So: why bother living out that version? Whatever swell archaeological discoveries I might make, let someone else. Let me try doing something unknown, chancy, unpredictable.

My daughter Sarah told me, in her early teens, "Dad, that was really stupid for you to drop out of Yale."

"But you wouldn't exist if I hadn't dropped out of Yale."

"You know what I mean. Anyway, a different version of me would exist."

My parents didn't try too hard to dissuade me from my crazy decision to abandon my path to success. They knew the more opposition I met, the more determined I'd get.

I had come up with the idea of playing creative music professionally. I would pursue this dream by moving to a city I'd never visited and knew little about, Chicago. What lured me there was the Association for the Advancement of Creative Musicians: the mythic AACM.

3-GOING TO CHICAGO

AUGUST 1979

Surprisingly, I didn't have to show up in Chicago cold. My friend Valerie Wattenberg—also an actor with the summer children's theater—turned out to have grown up in Oak Park. I stayed with her family the last week of August while apartment-hunting. Valerie's sister Melissa, and their friends Michael Edwalds and Peter Kruley, assigned themselves the job of looking out for me. This unanticipated support network made my start easy.

    I received well-meaning advice from the super at one of the buildings I called. In a soft, West Virginia accent, she said, "People will tell you Chicago is a cold city, and it's true if you carry a chip on your shoulder someone will knock it off. But if you walk around with a smile on your face, you'll find it's just a big country town."

    Uh-oh. I was the one at whom strangers in the street shouted, "Smile!"

A week later, Christine Bluhm hired me into her bookstore as a receiving clerk. My first regular job.

    Chris had worked in bookstores and libraries in Michigan, Minnesota, Wisconsin, and Illinois, while going to college and then graduate school in both art history and library science. She'd dropped out of the grad programs and was now climbing the ladder of a rapidly growing bookstore chain: she ran the new B. Dalton Bookseller across from the Water Tower, on Chicago's Magnificent Mile. The day before I showed up, she'd fired her previous receiving clerk, because another employee had found a box of books addressed by this receiver to his own apartment: the box was sitting out ready to be picked up by UPS.

A few days after Chris hired me, she took off for a one-week impulsive trip to Israel with her friend Doreet. When I asked her, on her return, about this sudden departure, she said she was always thinking about her next trip. Which, now, would be to Indonesia, in a year. I wasn't clear where Indonesia was.

In the basement, sitting at her desk near my receiving counter, on her daily lunch break, she'd ask me a question. While I discoursed, she'd eat. When I ran out of steam, she'd ask another. I explained creative music versus free jazz versus mainstream jazz; theater improv versus jazz improv; and the practical details of the world's coming anarchist utopia.

The Association for the Advancement of Creative Musicians was not in the phone book, but in the *Chicago Reader*, I found a concert listing for Steve and Iqua Colson. I was pretty sure they were AACM members, and I did find them in the phone book. Iqua Colson answered. I said I had moved to Chicago to join the AACM. She sounded surprised, and explained that you had to be nominated, by someone who knew you.

I went down to The Blue Gargoyle—near the University of Chicago—and caught a fabulous six-member ensemble called Inventions, led by Douglas Ewart, a multi-instrumentalist winds wizard. After the concert, I asked Douglas if I could jam with him. He seemed hesitant.

Bill Meade had once told me you could ask any musician for a lesson. He'd looked up guys in the New York City phone book, cold-called, and succeeded. Joe Henderson, Lee Konitz—real heavyweights. So, I thought to ask Douglas if instead of jamming, he'd give me a lesson. He said okay.

The next week, I was in his South Side apartment at 51st and Ellis.

On a table, I noticed a stack of flyers announcing a concert series. The AACM's printed tagline was "Great Black Music."

I'd thought of creative musicians as a racially-integrated community. Many of the creative-music and free-jazz records I owned had mixed line-ups. Also, I had a brochure from Creative Music Studio, in Woodstock, New York—founded by Karl Berger, Ornette Coleman and Don Cherry—where I'd considered taking classes, before deciding instead to move to Chicago. This brochure listed Black and white musicians teaching together, including quite a few AACM members.

I didn't ask Douglas about the AACM tagline.

We chatted a little, and then he suggested we play together. I was excited. After about twenty minutes, he said, "I hate to break us up, but I do have some work." He handed me a beginner's exercise book and said he'd like me to start on page one, with long tones. For every note on the horn, from the lowest to the highest, I was to produce an even, balanced, long tone. He'd like to see me next month. To clarify that he himself had been through such a discipline, he pointed out that all through this book there were markings with lesson dates, and his teacher's initials, AB. Douglas had used the book in '65. His teacher was Anthony Braxton—who, of course, I knew was an internationally famous AACM genius.

I accepted the book and brought it back north to my studio apartment in Uptown. I felt a little humiliated that I was supposed to begin at the beginning, but I did wish to become an AACM member, and I was willing to do as I was told, if Douglas Ewart was the person telling me. Questioning authority has its limits.

I was on the eighth floor. The first day I began playing long tones, after five minutes, a thumping was heard beneath my feet. I thought it was the water pipes.

The thumping got louder.

Shortly, a banging commenced on my door. I opened, to find a lady with a broom. She said she'd been banging on her ceiling with the broom-handle, but I hadn't stopped, so, she'd had to come up.

I explained I'd been assigned long tones. This didn't interest her. I closed the door and continued my long tones. Twenty minutes later, there was more banging. This time, it was the broom lady and the super. The super said to stop.

I negotiated limited practice hours.

I didn't always remember my limits, and the neighbor used her broom on and off all year.

* * *

THE MUSIC THIEF

One Friday night, I headed south to a jam session on 51st Street. The El train came to a halt on an overpass. Electricity problem. We were in mid-air over a deep railyard.

There were three other people in my car: two men sitting a few seats behind me, and a man sitting across from me, by himself. The two guys behind started chatting: "White people own this El. They're the ones who run this damned thing. Like everything white, always breaking down."

"Yes, we should burn this train down."

"Yeah, we should take that white kid there and throw him out the window."

"We could stuff him out, let him fall all the way down."

"We ought to do that, let all the white people know what we think of their white things."

I was seated squarely in the middle of the car. I stayed still, head down.

The train lurched, made its way to the next station, and the two men got off, grumbling.

The guy across from me said, "Hey man, I want you to know that if those guys had done what they were talking about, I would have fought alongside you. No-one should talk that way. Even if a man is white, he's still a man."

I could hardly speak. I managed, "Gee, thanks man." He got off at the next stop, and I continued to 51st Street.

The club was packed, and a lot of guys were lined up to play. One after another, they showed their stuff. It was fast, mainstream jazz. All these musicians were technically proficient. I was ashamed—and bored. I had zero discipline when it came to the hours you had to invest practicing scales, arpeggios, and patterns to play this way. And these guys all sounded the same. Why had I come?

After an hour, I left, without having played.

I felt depressed and went to an all-night cafeteria. I noticed that the guy sitting in the next booth was not looking good. He opened his mouth, and a river of food oozed out.

I jumped up, ran behind, and gave him the Heimlich maneuver, or as close to one as I could invent. He belched more food and started gasping. When he recovered his breath, he said, "Gee, thanks man."

I must have missed the last train. After standing on the platform for half an hour I gave up and caught a bus. This took me only as far as 35th Street. I had to get out and wait for a connecting bus. It was two-thirty AM.

The bus came; I went to the back. A stop later, two guys got on; they also came to the back, sitting behind me.

I had my soprano sax in its black leatherette case. One guy asked, "Hey man, what are you doing here, so late? What's in that bag? A pool cue? A rifle?"

"My horn." I unzipped to show it. "I was at a jam. What are you doing here?"

"I'm having a great time. Relaxing, back in the States. Traveling here and there. Gotta renew my connections, get ready for my next trip."

"Oh yeah, where you going?"

"Germany, man. All those army bases: they need their horse. Every year I spend five or six months—supplying, supplying. Then I come home, arrange some more."

"Wow, so, you supply the soldiers in Germany with heroin?"

"Pretty much, that's what I do. Been doing it for a long time, too. You know who this man is?" He gestured to the other guy.

"Who?"

"This is my bodyguard!" They both laughed.

As the two stood up to get off, the second guy asked, "Hey, man, you got a psychologist?"

"No, why?"

"You need to have your head examined, coming out this time of night. It's dangerous!"

Sunday afternoon a few weeks later, I headed to The Copher Box, on the far South Side, to catch Kahil El'Zabar and the Ethnic Heritage Ensemble. It was a two-hour bus-ride. I got to see the whole city.

The Copher Box could have turned me away, since I was underage; maybe they let me in because they were so surprised. I sat up front and drank ginger ale.

Kahil El'Zabar's African drumming and kalimba playing were a transport, Ed Wilkerson's testimony on tenor sax was blistering, Light Henry Huff was ethereal on soprano. Then, the second-set surprise was singer Luba Rashik, a passionate, political poet.

After the show, I asked Kahil if he'd jam with me. He was kind and gave me his phone number. Over the next two months, I spoke with him a few times. He was always too busy, but never said no. I gave up. I was not as good as Ed Wilkerson or Light Henry Huff; why was I wasting his time?

I started theater improv classes with Josephine Forsberg, who was running Players Workshop of Second City. Fifteen actors played games conjuring relationships, physicalizing settings and convening scenic realities on the fly, while Jo side-coached. Jo once complimented me with, "Good sensuality!"

Jo had founded Players Workshop twenty years before, when Paul Sills was still running Second City—the theater that has spurred the rise of modern comic improv, launching Elaine May, Ed Asner, Alan Arkin, and so many *Saturday Night Live* performers like John Belushi and Bill Murray. I didn't know then that in the forties, Paul Sills' mother Viola Spolin, while working with immigrants at Hull House, had invented the precursor to the Second City improv technique as a children's theater curriculum called creative dramatics. I'd used Spolin's theater games in New Haven.

The next month, I auditioned for Earth Theater, and Rudolf Munro—aka Long John Silver—hired me to tour schools in *Treasure Island,* playing Jim Hawkins. A month after that, with singer/songwriter Ellen Rosner, I co-founded the five-piece folk-rock band Fine Tuning. At our Café Barbarossa gig, the stage was so small, I had to play my sax solos standing on a table. I loved that. We weren't invited back.

My manager Chris and I went out: we saw Rick Cluchey at the Goodman Theater, performing Samuel Beckett's *Krapp's Last Tape.* Cluchey had become a dramatist while incarcerated at San Quentin, turned on by a visiting troupe's performance of Beckett's *Waiting for Godot.* Cluchey's prison-theater work was so impressive that his sentence was commuted; he went to Europe and became Beckett's disciple. His Beckett-directed *Krapp's Last Tape* performance was stunning.

Afterward, Chris and I shared a bus; my place was north of hers, on the same Sheridan bus-line.

She invited me to get off at her stop, to see her apartment.

Scanning her records, I saw saxophonist Arthur Blythe's newest release, *Lenox Avenue Breakdown*. I'd bought it six months before, in New Haven. Then, I saw a boxed set of Carla Bley's three-record jazz opera, *Escalator Over the Hill*. I owned a later pressing, with an ordinary album sleeve. I loved Bley's compositions, with their crazy Paul Haines lyrics. Chris said she'd bought EOTH in '73.

This woman had great taste.

That night, I lost my virginity.

Our Dalton held a couple of author events that year. We had photographer Ansel Adams a few weeks after I arrived, and a few months later, after Chris and I had started dating, and decided I'd join her trip to Indonesia, Harrison Salisbury came through to autograph *Travels Across America.* I was in the basement. I didn't know who he was: the *New York Times* reporter who'd covered trouble spots around the world for fifty years. Chris ran downstairs and told me I had to meet him.

Chris told Salisbury we were going to Indonesia. He was tall, silver-haired, distinguished, but with a glint in his eye. He said if we were going to Southeast Asia, we had to go to Burma. Our travels began to blossom outwards. Why only go to Indonesia?

*   *   *

My co-worker, artist Paul Berlanga, mentioned that his wife Mary Phelan, a professional portraitist, was interested in painting me while I improvised. I spent eight Sunday mornings at their place, noodling on tenor sax, while Mary created a passionate, impressionist artwork. Then she gave me the painting, refusing payment!

There was a staff party after work. My relationship with Chris was taboo, she being my boss, plus—I'd learned to my surprise—nearly nine years older than me. Since I wasn't seeing her every night, I hadn't touched base; I assumed she'd arrive separately, and we'd spend the evening pretending we weren't together.

All twenty of the Dalton staff came, but not Chris. Evidently, she hadn't been invited. I was startled to hear cutting comments about her. Boss-is-a-jerk stuff. I'd never heard any of these people talk that way. I'd assumed everyone liked Chris. She'd assembled a fun team of artistically-minded people, and she always spoke highly of them to me. She'd remained friends with former employees.

Over the next few months, as our relationship deepened, it became harder for me to work at the store and pretend I was just her employee. Also—several times, we were almost found out.

I cut my hours, then in June, quit.

One Sunday afternoon in early July, I headed for an audition at a theater company on the South Side. I'd seen the notice in the *Chicago Reader*. I figured if I got off at the 35th Street El station, I'd be a few blocks from my Indiana Avenue destination.

Descending the steps from the train platform, carrying my sax, in a crowd of people, I heard someone yelling, "Help, murder! Help! They're killing me!" The voice seemed to be coming from inside the station. As I came down the final flight of stairs, I saw a burly white man in shabby clothes standing in front of another, bigger white man who was down on the ground on top of a third man. This third man was Black. He was pinned flat on his stomach. There was a pool of blood all around his head, which was turned sideways toward the crowd passing through the station. It was the man on the ground who was yelling, "Murder! Help!" The big guy on top of him pulled his head up and slammed it against the concrete.

Everyone in the station seemed to be ignoring the scene.

I was pretty freaked out, but I went up to the guy who was standing guard—he was half a head taller than me and twice as wide—and said, "Hey, stop that."

With authority in his voice he barked, "Keep walking, this is police business."

I didn't believe him. The two white men looked like regular slobs. The Black guy yelled again, "They're killing me!" The guy on top—a monster of a man—punched him hard in the back of his neck. I now saw the Black guy's arms were pulled behind him: the white guy was sitting on the Black guy's arms. The pool of blood extended several feet in every direction.

Most of the people who'd come down the steps had passed through the station—I was the only rider left.

I saw there was a payphone near the front entrance. I hurried to it and called nine-one-one. I spoke to an operator and told her what I was seeing. She said she'd send police over right away. As I hung up, three uniformed officers and one man in street clothes came into the station past me and walked over to the standing white man. They started talking together in a friendly way.

I felt powerless to do anything else, and I knew I'd be late for the audition if I hung around. I'd called nine-one-one. I could see there was even a ticket agent in the booth who wasn't doing anything about the violence. I left the station and started walking east along 35th Street. When I got to Indiana Avenue, I turned south, toward the address for the theater.

It was a hot day. There were lots of people on front steps, hanging around parked cars, standing in groups on corners. I was the focus of everyone's attention. "Hey honky! Whatchya doin' here? Get out of here or we're gonna kick your ass!" "Hey honky, who do you think you are? Run!"

I tried not to make eye contact. I considered crossing to the other side of Indiana, but there were lots of people over there interested in me. I moved faster. The yelling continued, but no one made a move—they only threatened. I realized I was not going to this audition, and I couldn't turn around and go back to the El past all those angry people.

I could see there was another El station a few blocks south, at 40th Street. I started running, and a minute later I was breathlessly climbing the stairs to the platform. I took the train back to the North Side.

(I didn't learn till years later of that Bronzeville neighborhood's battles against white gangbangers, who used underpasses to sneak from their Bridgeport neighborhood through the great wall of the Dan Ryan Expressway—built that way by Mayor Richard J. Daley so as to insulate his white ethnic fiefdom from the Black South Side.)

That night, I told Chris what had happened in the El station. I assumed I'd stumbled on a common scene. White cops beat up Black guy. Horrible, because no-one even considered it exceptional.

That week, I didn't have any rehearsals or classes. I spent the days alone, practicing music, and writing. I didn't own a TV, so I wasn't paying attention to the news.

Friday night, I went to a party at Michael Edwalds' apartment in Oak Park. I overheard some people discussing a rumor of a police-brutality killing. I broke into their conversation, and they were surprised I didn't know. The police were denying stories that the death of a man in custody was the result of brutality. The arrest had taken place the previous Sunday, on the South Side.

"I saw that." I told my story, and Michael's guests said my version of the events matched some, but not all of the story confirmed by police. They also said a call was out for witnesses, but so far, no witnesses had turned up.

"But there were fifty people who got off the train when I did!" I couldn't believe not a single person who'd seen this beating had stepped forward.

I realized suddenly that any Black person would be risking their life to stand up against the Chicago police, especially if they lived in the neighborhood where that beating had taken place. I was young and white, with no local family to be terrorized. I wasn't from Chicago, so I didn't have any history of being scared by the Chicago police. I decided to tell my story to whoever would listen.

Michael suggested I should start by calling police headquarters directly, since it was the police who'd put out the call for witnesses. I went into his bedroom, looked in the phone book and called the main number. I was told to call Office of Professional Services. I did and spoke to someone who was very dubious. We made an appointment for an OPS officer to visit me.

On Monday afternoon, two men in business suits came to my apartment. I told them my story, and they took notes. They asked me a bunch of questions about myself. They said someone from the state's attorney's office would call.

The state's attorney's office asked me to come to them. I went downtown and told the assistant state's attorney the same story I'd given the OPS guys.

Chris heard on news-radio the next day, in the bookstore, that an eyewitness had come forward in the 35th Street El case.

That would be me.

A few days later, I received a call from the assistant state's attorney. "Mr. Laties? We're obliged to inform you that we have provided your address to the attorney for the defense."

"What does that mean?"

"The officers who arrested the offender on the El have an attorney. By law, our office is required to turn over information about witnesses to this attorney."

"So, the cops have my address?"

"That is possible."

Now I was scared. Those murderers had not been charged or arrested. I was the only eyewitness who'd come forward.

Three days later, I was walking from my apartment down Clarendon Drive. Every evening, I'd make this walk from my place to Chris' apartment, ten blocks south on Agatite.

I was thinking hard, looking at the ground, as I often did when I walked.

Clarendon was near the lakefront—green space with high-rises. There was no one around.

Someone was in my way.

I looked up, and there they were. Both of them, blocking me. The burly man who'd said, "Keep walking, this is police business," and, next to him, the huge guy who'd been hitting the Black man.

They were looming. The first guy grimaced, leaned toward me, and, in a slow voice, said, "Don't worry about us."

Monster-man opened his eyes wide and growled, "We're just CRAZY!"

I whipped around them like a jackrabbit and tore off down the street. Running from the cops!

I wove back and forth, as I remembered you should if you think you might get shot at. Four-hundred-yard dash!

I ran for blocks, cutting through alleys, stopping behind dumpsters. He that runs away, lives!

They must have been watching me the past few days, plotting their threat.

When I got to Chris' house, I called Office of Professional Services.

OPS refused to take my report. I was mistaken about who had spoken to me. The words had not been a threat: "Don't worry about us."

I didn't call the assistant state's attorney. He was the one who'd given the cops my address. I was on my own, here.

Chris and I had already bought one-way tickets to Indonesia. Good timing. The next day, I went to Morrie Mages sports store and got a baseball bat. Fun to swing. It started coming with me everywhere.

I changed my habits. When going around town, I stayed among people.

Chris heard on the radio that another eyewitness had come forward. Phew.

A couple of weeks later, the assistant state's attorney called to say there were several witnesses, and the trial would take months to prepare. I told him I was leaving for Indonesia and wasn't sure when I'd be back. He said I should keep in touch; when the prosecution needed me, I'd have to return.

The year before, a police brutality trial near Miami resulting in acquittal had sparked the Liberty City riots. My friends guessed the state's attorney would make sure this Chicago trial took place in mid-winter, to reduce the duration of similar riots, in case of police acquittal.

Radio reported that those cops had now been suspended from the force but given jobs as Teamsters. Everywhere I went, my eyes were peeled: I kept thinking I saw one or the other, but they didn't confront me again.

Scared of my baseball bat, probably.

* * *

A week before we left town, I visited Paul and Mary to say goodbye. I was surprised to see that Mary was in pain. They were short of cash for a medical procedure.

I solicited money from Dad: payment for the portrait. In the Los Angeles airport, an hour before we boarded for Indonesia, I dropped the thousand-dollar check into a mailbox. She surely couldn't refuse if I was ten-thousand miles away.

THE MUSIC THIEF

4-THERE AND BACK AGAIN

OCTOBER 1980

From the stifling heat and crowds of Jakarta—ignoring all the guys asking, "Where are you going?" and, "Can I practice my English?"—we fled to the cool uplands of Bandung, where I wailed on sax inside the rim of a volcano. Train to Jogjakarta, where we visited with my friend teaching English there, Mark Elder—who informed us that the question, "Where are you going?" was a polite greeting and we should respond with, "Jalan-jalan," which meant "Walking-walking."

    Evening bus to Surabaya, seated in front of Mark's friend Ted Fishman, who warned me to stop playing kalimba because other passengers were murmuring their annoyance. To Bali by ferry—playing sax quietly on deck—then spending several days in the arts village of Ubud, listening to gamelan orchestra till late, kept awake overnight by hundreds of barking dogs.

    Back to Jakarta—day-tripping to a gamelan-making village to buy a reyong pot-gong I then mailed off to Douglas Ewart—ending our month in Indonesia crammed for three days with eight-hundred others on board the three-story KM Tampomas—where a guy yelled I had ignored him in Jakarta when all he wanted was to practice English—

finally docking in super-clean Singapore, which seemed to me a hyper-obsessive London without the high culture.

Hitchhiking through Malaysia, a Chinese policeman took us to Penang, complaining about government mistreatment of Chinese businessmen and the ending of English-language classes in the schools.

Train to Bangkok, city of horrific traffic jams and vibrant markets surrounding golden temples. Bus to Chiang Mai, where, after a rat zipped across our bed, we switched hotels at midnight, the next day renting bikes to explore the countryside.

Chris had quit her Dalton job—she'd had it with the corporate career—so, we weren't under the gun. We'd vaguely planned to travel for two months, but as we drifted through Thailand and our money ran low, we changed our minds and headed for Japan, where, my *FightBack* friend Bill Heinrich had told me, as he'd done the year before, we could find good-paying work teaching English.

Tokyo in December was snowy. We'd seen a handwritten notice in Bangkok's Malaysia Hotel recommending a private rooming-house called Michiko's, and when we arrived at Narita airport, we called the number. Michiko gave us directions. Arriving in the evening at Daitabashi station, we walked down narrow lanes past dozens of brightly-lit shops. Karen Carpenter Christmas songs were pumping through a Dunkin Donuts loudspeaker. We stopped to buy sweaters.

A day before, in the Bangkok paper, we'd read John Lennon was killed. At Michiko's, Beatles music was playing. We joined a dozen travelers from around the world remembering Lennon.

Michiko's guests told us we'd been smart not to line up jobs. Schools that advertised for teachers in the US made you sign a one-year contract, at half the going rate, but if you just showed up, you could earn more. We should ask twenty dollars an hour to start, and after a bit of experience, fifty. That we didn't speak Japanese was a plus, since schools wanted teachers with whom students couldn't shift the conversation from English. The main thing was our American accents; Japanese businessmen needed to learn these, for success with American counterparts.

Michiko's was a homey place. She'd spent a couple of years abroad: Europe and New York. Because she'd lived outside Japan, no one would hire her, so she had to be self-employed. She enjoyed foreigners, so this business was perfect. There were only a few other hostels in Tokyo, and—especially because it was cheaper than a hotel—her place was always full. But she didn't have a license and warned us that as we came and went, we should be unobtrusive.

The next day, on a tourist-information-center bulletin board, we saw a notice for an apartment being leased by an American, in the Koenji neighborhood. Dave turned out to have been teaching English in Japan for twelve years. Each time he moved, he'd retained his former apartment, so he now had a business sub-leasing to other Americans. The room was tiny, with no bathroom: shared toilet down the hall, public bathhouse down the street. Living like the locals.

Chris and I scoured English-language newspapers and found jobs by responding to want-ads. I was hired to teach Tuesdays and Thursdays in the suburb of Fuchu, by a guy named Vivoo. Like Michiko, he'd traveled abroad on his own—in his case, through Asia to Afghanistan, then working as a cook for several months in Germany—and this worldly experience had rendered him unemployable at home, so he was running his own business. My afternoon classes would be with children, the evening ones with adults. I got an additional job with Stanford Institute of English Conversation. Between the two gigs, I was set to earn several-thousand dollars a month. Chris landed work at a junior college for girls, and at two corporations: a pharmaceuticals firm and the downtown headquarters of Mitsubishi.

We signed up for classes in Japanese culture with teachers we'd found through the tourist-information center. In this way, we'd qualify for cultural visas, which would permit us to work legally. Chris would be studying contemporary pottery with a young artist named Mika, and traditional pottery with raku-yaki specialist Sakio Baba. I opted to study shakuhachi.

I'd never heard a shakuhachi, I only knew it was a kind of Japanese flute. I'd found a listing for Soke Chikuyu-sha as a school that accepted Westerners. I'd called and made an appointment to meet the director.

Kawase Junsuke III turned out to have recently taught for a year at Wesleyan University: this experience had made him interested in having a few foreign students.

I didn't know then that he was one of the most internationally-esteemed shakuhachi masters: the hereditary leader of the largest group of Kinko-school players. In this case, school doesn't mean just an educational establishment, but also a style of music. The musical notation can only be read by people trained in this style. The songs, embellishments, method of flute construction, placement and size of holes are all particular.

Kawase Junsuke requested that I promise not to play anything on the shakuhachi other than the Kinko music he would be teaching. Since I wanted to study with him even more after he'd said this peculiar thing, I agreed. It seemed doubtful that I wouldn't improvise on the instrument, though.

After he told me a little about his time at Wesleyan, he played. I'd had no idea how gorgeous the instrument would sound. So lush and romantic and subtle. He had incredible breath control; his notes were oozing and wavy. His dynamics, the idiosyncratic breathiness—I was amazed.

He said it would take one year of playing the public style—sankyoku—before I'd be allowed to study the secret style of honkyoku. So, I'd have to promise to stay with the school for at least one year. Again, I promised—though Chris and I had arrived in Japan with plans to stay for a few months.

He took me to a workshop connected to the main building, where other musicians were making shakuhachis. This school made its own instruments! He selected one, and I paid him two hundred dollars. I brought it back, and Chris was shocked and upset when I told her I'd blown two hundred dollars of our money on my new flute, and we had to stay in Tokyo for a year.

Then I tried to play the thing. No way. It was completely different from the silver flute I could so easily handle. I couldn't figure out how Kawase Junsuke had gotten sound out of this open tube of bamboo. I tried to visualize his lip placement, but it didn't make sense. True, I could get a note by blowing across the top, like I blew a beer bottle. That was wrong. I looked forward to my first lesson, when Kawase Junsuke would show me how to hold the instrument to my lip and tell me how to finger.

When the day came, he sat me on the floor in front of a little table, sat himself on the other side, put a sheet of unreadable music between us, and proceeded to play what evidently was on the page. Then he waited. He maintained silence. I understood I wasn't supposed to speak. I tried to do what he had, failing to get any sound.

He repeated. I did see the instrument was jammed against his chin, so his lips were at the farther edge of the flute's top. I tried to copy, but I could feel my lower lip wasn't long enough to cover the opening. I still couldn't get a sound, but the breathiness sounded promising.

We spent half an hour, him playing the scale, me struggling to copy. Then he got up and bowed, and I did too—and my knees hurt, from scrunching.

I left, realizing I wasn't going to get questions answered, explanations, or any verbal instruction. Just the opportunity to copy. Really different from a lesson in the US.

After a few sessions, Kawase Junsuke passed me off to another teacher, whose playing was also gorgeous, and who also communicated by playing. I was gradually introduced to a complex system of notation, and I had to deduce what the scrawls must mean. It was helpful I could read Western music, since I was able to learn by analogy.

One thing I found fascinating was that so many of the important elements of the style—things the teacher would repeat over and over until I had them approximately right—were not reflected on the written page.

THE MUSIC THIEF

I did get to pose some of my pressing questions a few months later to another American who was studying shakuhachi. I asked about my embouchure—lip position—which I was concerned was not right, but for which I was receiving no corrective advice. He said shakuhachi players developed their own sounds and unique embouchures. He'd seen a book of photographs of famous shakuhachi players. Some held their flutes vertically to the ground, others held them horizontally from their bodies. Some contorted their lips, others maintained an even mouth as if kissing.

Within each school, some masters had a rich, full tone, while others had a breathy sound. None was wrong.

The shakuhachi has a singular history. It's a Zen instrument, played alone: it isn't for concerts or audiences. It's supposed to suggest the sound of an empty bell. Players seek "yugen" which translates—poorly—as profundity. The famous historical period of shakuhachi playing was the seventeenth through nineteenth centuries. A sect called the komuso, who wore baskets upside down on their heads, covering their faces, played shakuhachi as they wandered the countryside. They were mendicant monks—holy beggars. After the Tokugawas came to power and stripped samurai knights of the right to bear swords, some became spies, dressing as komuso monks. With baskets masking their heads, no one knew their identities. One minute a samurai spy would be playing his thick shakuhachi, the next, he'd be wielding the bamboo flute as a weapon, whacking his enemy. Musical warriors of Zen.

* * *

Practicing my quiet shakuhachi in our apartment was fine, but sax was another matter. My first time, ten minutes in, there was a knock. I opened the door to a diminutive, bowing police officer. I bowed in return. He smiled, pointed at my sax, cocked his head and raised his eyebrows. I nodded. He bowed again. I bowed too and closed the door. I put away the horn.

Police here were different.

My job at Vivoo's involved a fifteen-minute walk from the Fuchu train station; the route passed open fields traversed by a railway bridge. I started bringing my sax; I'd arrive in Fuchu an hour early and practice under the bridge.

One afternoon as I approached my spot, I heard a free-jazz tenor sax player's uninterrupted barrage. I quickened my pace, took out my horn, and added my erratic, quirky stuff to his volcanism. He didn't acknowledge me, just kept up the circular breathing—remarkable, considering how hard he was blowing. Douglas Ewart had shown me how, but I'd been too undisciplined to develop much skill.

Ten minutes later, the tenor player stopped. I did too. He had no English and I no Japanese. His name was Junji. He named his favorite player—Evan Parker—who I knew was the British circular-breathing tenor-sax master. Junji wrote down when and where his group would soon be performing. Then he had to leave.

A week later, Chris and I went to hear Junji's trio: sax, bass and drums. The music was powerful and uncompromising. I would have died to enter this scene—but Junji didn't invite me and I couldn't communicate my desire.

I needed to learn Japanese. I studied phrase books and dictionaries while riding the subway. It took a few months, but eventually I was conversing.

I continued to practice sax under the railway bridge, hoping Junji would come, but we didn't cross paths.

For several months, Chris and I loved our lives. Tokyo was constantly surprising. At first, we thought we'd stumbled into a New York of the future, everything technological. So many things American seemed to have been adapted and integrated and weirdly elaborated.

Gradually, we realized locals experienced their city differently. For instance, on the subway, the cars were unbearably crowded: you couldn't move. And silent: no one said a word. Claustrophobic. But, when I asked one of my students at Vivoo's—Mr. Takahashi—what he thought about when he was jammed into a train-car, he said he closed his eyes and visualized himself on his native island of Sapporo, alone in a pine forest.

An American teacher at Stanford Institute who'd lived in Japan for a few years told me the Japanese had a saying about Americans in Japan: "The American who visits Japan for one day will write a book. The American who visits Japan for one week will write an article. The American who visits Japan for one month will write a page. The American who visits Japan for one year will write a paragraph. The American who visits Japan for five years will write a sentence. The American who visits Japan for ten years will write a word. The American who spends a lifetime in Japan will write nothing."

My students told me fascinating things about Japanese culture: funeral practices, life in Manchuria in the thirties, keeping pet beetles, drinking rituals, arranged marriage systems, and what things you were allowed to say in English but never in Japanese. One thing that became clear was that apparently-American influence was not considered that way. With Chinese culture before, and now with American, the Japanese took what they could use, re-aligning what was borrowed to a Japanese meaning.

Japan was the most unique culture, with the most unique history, and the most unique people, and the most unique language, in the world. Ever. And unique meant best.

America on the other hand was known as "the sick society." Everyone was out for himself. Individualism was all that counted, which meant the group was at odds. No culture could be considered healthy that had its people constantly competing with one another. In Japan, "The nail that sticks out will get hammered down."

Chris and I began to get tired of living in Japan.

Japan was also super-misogynistic, and this women-are-lesser-beings attitude began to wear on Chris' nerves. I couldn't blame her for getting fed up with Japanese men. She was spending fifteen hours a week in corporate offices trying to get identically blue-suited salarymen to converse in fractured English. When she accepted one group's offer of a beer after class, her reward—at the bar—was a lecture about her duty to return to America and fulfill her biological destiny as a mother.

For myself, I'd found it peculiar sitting next to guys reading violent manga in the subway—with storylines involving the rape and dismemberment of women—while right next to them, schoolgirls perused romantic manga showing cute men and pretty women struggling in relationships.

It was something beyond the anti-individualism and misogyny that made me uneasy though. I had trouble putting my finger on it. Just: everyone was so nice. Overwhelmingly polite. Absolutely welcoming. It got to feel like I was being held at a distance because I might bite. Even people I was spending a lot of time with acted this way.

I began to wonder what they were secretly thinking.

One afternoon at Stanford Institute, I subbed for another teacher's class of fifteen senior executives. Their English was weak. I went around the group, having each person introduce himself, asking questions I'd used in my class for junior executives: "Do you have any brothers or sisters? Where were you born?"

One white-haired man answered, "I'm from Yokohama." His neighbors acted impressed that he'd spoken an English sentence.

"Yokohama? I have been to Yokohama. I like Yokohama." The man laughed.

"What did your father do for a living?"

He didn't understand. His neighbor translated into his ear. He responded to the neighbor in Japanese.

"He says, his family owned a bathhouse."

"A bathhouse? I love going to the bathhouse. Does your family still own the bathhouse?"

The neighbor translated, and the white-haired man again responded in Japanese.

"He says, his family doesn't own the bathhouse."

"Did they sell the bathhouse?"

Now several of the men were talking in Japanese. "He says, the bathhouse isn't there."

"Why not?"

The men's conversation was taking over. I interrupted, trying to bring them back to English. "What happened to the bathhouse?"

The neighbor said, "No bathhouse now. No more bathhouse."

"Yes, I see. But what happened to the bathhouse?"

A third man said, "Bathhouse went away," and made a gesture, raising his hand up, then dropping it suddenly.

"Went away? How could a bathhouse go away?"

Several men were making the rising-dropping hand gesture, with sound effects. "Boom!" "Pum!" "America boom!"

"Oh! Americans bombed the bathhouse during the war!"

Many men smiled and nodded, several of them saying, "Yes—America—bomb." They seemed pleased I was showing signs of intelligence.

"He says, all his family died."

I found myself bowing my head several times quickly and saying, "I'm so sorry."

All these older men bowed their heads to me. "You are young." "We are sorry, too." "America, Japan, everyone is sorry."

I noticed that the Stanley Kubrick film *Dr. Strangelove* was playing in Ikebukuro. We'd each seen it before, but neither of us remembered the plot. I recalled it as a hilarious anti-war satire. At Yale, during the closing credits, everyone had sung along with "We'll Meet Again."

We entered the theater at the last minute. It was packed with five hundred people; we slid into seats up front. Japanese subtitles—not dubbed, thank goodness.

I wondered how the humor was coming across in written translation. So many of the jokes depended on knowledge of the paranoid nineteen-fifties American cultural context and Cold War arms race with Russia.

I felt how strange it was for us to be watching this acerbic American anti-war film in Japan, the country America blew up during World War II. Whispering together, Chris and I realized that in this theater, we'd become Ugly Americans: living symbols of the unspoken American/Japanese conversation, since—because we'd arrived after the entire Japanese audience was seated, then taken seats up front—the whole audience must have noted our entrance.

Nobody in the theater laughed during the entire film. So far removed from its original context, *Dr. Strangelove* was being misread as an expression of American eagerness to fight total war. Some scenes could be interpreted as crassly humorous, but the overall message looked deadly serious: don't mess with the US because we're crazy.

At the end, when dozens of nuclear bombs were exploding, and "We'll Meet Again" was playing, I think nobody breathed. Anyway, we didn't.

*   *   *

Relaxing in the Stanford Institute teacher's lounge, I opened the international edition of *Time Magazine* and almost jumped. There was Maya Lin, smiling.

Last saw her at that house party, two years ago.

Her design for the Vietnam Veteran's Memorial would be built, in Washington, DC?

Wait—there was going to be a memorial about the Vietnam War?

But didn't the whole country want to forget that embarrassment?

Maya would make them face the truth?

The war sure had reached her now.

Wow.

We were twenty-one. She was in the spotlight: the conscience of our generation. I felt electric. Scared for her, and hopeful.

Had she been interested in me?

Missed that moment.

Sunday afternoon, Harajuku Station was filled with teen James Deans, Marilyn Monroes, and Elvis Presleys. From the elevated platform, I came down the steps looking for Sonomi, who'd invited me to have coffee.

Vivoo had warned me never to accept such an offer from one of our students: they'd be getting a free English lesson and we needed them to pay. But a week ago—just before class at Stanford Institute—I'd encountered my student Sonomi at a noodle shop. She'd started a conversation in Japanese that I'd felt proud to navigate.

"Do you like Japan?"

"Yes, I like it."

"I don't like Japan."

"Why not?"

"I want to move to Northern Canada."

Sonomi was about my age and—unlike the other women in my classes—rarely smiled. I'd replied, "I like Canada. But Northern Canada—it's very cold in Northern Canada."

"I like the cold."

A few days later, when Sonomi had asked if I'd meet her in Harajuku, I'd agreed. This school wasn't Vivoo's after all.

Sonomi rushed through the fashion-district cosplay crowd, took my hand, and pulled me onto the sidewalk. We started walking.

In Japanese, she asked, "Do you have a girlfriend?"

This was a surprise. "Yes."

We continued walking.

"Will you get married?"

"No, we will live together our whole lives, but not get married."

"Why won't you get married?"

"We think getting married is not good."

Pressing through the crowd of fifties pop icons, we hadn't been looking at each other. Now she stopped and addressed me directly, "If you don't get married, you won't live your lives together. Do you like me?"

It took a few seconds to understand what she'd said—and I was unprepared. I'd guessed the reason for our coffee date was so she could ask me about traveling outside Japan; maybe she needed to escape parental pressure into an arranged marriage.

"You are a very nice person, but—I have a girlfriend and I don't live in Northern Canada."

We'd walked two blocks. She pressed a square of paper into my hand and ran slowly down the sidewalk—dodging leather-jacketed Elvises and blond-wigged Marilyns—back toward Harajuku Station.

I unfolded the letter. Handwritten in English was a poetic confession of love that projected our life together in Northern Canada.

I ran slowly after her, past James Dean and Judy Garland. "Sonomi!"

She maintained her half-block lead. I caught up on the elevated platform, but she moved away. When the train came, we entered separate cars.

"Just marry her. What did you think would happen?"

"I don't know what I thought."

"Well, I'm leaving. You should stay."

"I don't want to stay without you."

"You signed up for your year of shakuhachi, you're speaking Japanese and making friends; you just stay."

All the longtime English teachers like our landlord Dave and the guys at Stanford Institute had Japanese wives.

We agreed to leave in two months. When I broke the news to my teachers and my students, several asked, "When will you return?"

"I don't know."

"One year?"

"Not one year, no."

"Two years?"

"Mmm. Not two years."

"Three years?"

"Maybe three years."

In school, Sonomi gave no sign anything had passed between us, but I suspected she continued to obsess over me. At our last class, she gave me a gift: a beautiful kimono doll.

Too big to pack. We left it on the train to the airport.

We got to Burma in October. At the base of Mandalay Hill, we sat on the ground chatting with two transgender priests who looked like Mick Jagger and Keith Richard. After exchanging gifts under the watchful eyes of dozens of tiny, bright-colored gods on a flower-petal-covered altar, while five ladies whirled to an oboe-and-gong orchestra, I smoked my first cigarette ever: pressed on me by Mick.

I never imagined I'd be hooked for decades.

An hour later, and fifteen-hundred steps up the temple mountain—in Sutaungpyei Pagoda—Chris wandered past rows of golden Buddhas, while I sent slow sax tones over the landscape.

A fortune teller approached. Examining my palm, she said, "You will have four children, and live to be eighty-eight." Nice: my longevity had improved since New York. She looked up happily to deliver the real news, "You will obtain a position with the civil service."

A few minutes later I was relieved to hear that Chris, too, would have four children and live to be eighty-eight, while also enjoying the lucky life of a civil servant.

*   *   *

But—Chris' real dream was to one day open her own bookstore, and, while we were in Konorak, on the west coast of India, during a week of wandering conversation, we decided to create her bookstore together.

We'd come by train from Calcutta to Bhubaneswar, then taken a bus to the coast. Each morning, we would walk the twenty minutes to an exquisite beach on the Bay of Bengal. Running into the surf, we were lifted, carried, and slammed back onto the stingingly grainy sand. In the afternoon, we'd explore the massive, erotically carved Chariot of the Sun temple. After dinner, I'd sit on the temple walls playing sax until the mosquitoes drove me inside. Then we'd get stoned, courtesy of an English couple named Richard and Victoria who made a living in southern France renovating old houses.

We figured if we could travel for a year together, we could do anything. Certainly, open a bookstore. We'd saved ten-thousand dollars in Tokyo. We calculated we could afford to open a newsstand in Paris.

Before that, though—we took the train back to Calcutta, then flew past mountains to Kathmandu. We rented bikes and found our way to a bookshop selling trekking maps.

We caught the bus to Pokhara, jammed in with families, sacks of vegetables, rugs, hardware, and chickens. It was a five-hour, bumpy ride, and Chris was looking faint. By the time we reached Pokhara, she could barely walk, but she begged me to find her a chicken sandwich.

"Why do you want a chicken sandwich? They don't have sandwiches here."

"Andy, please, just get me a chicken sandwich. I have to have a chicken sandwich."

We took an awful room in the closest hotel, right next to the bus station. Cement floors with a squat toilet down the hall. Chris lay on the bed while I went out and inquired of street vendors after a chicken sandwich. I found a little restaurant where a lady prepared something possibly resembling one—but when I returned to our room, Chris couldn't down a bite.

By eleven PM I was feeling terrible too: stomach cramps, dizziness. In the middle of the night we were both repeatedly rushing to the toilet with diarrhea and vomiting. We reached a point where we couldn't make it down the hall; we had to use our two cooking pots for shitting and puking.

I struggled with a flashlight to read in the health section of our Lonely Planet guidebook, *Southeast Asia on a Shoestring*—which we'd been using since Indonesia—searching for a diagnosis. I found it: dysentery. The intensity and speed of onset suggested the bacillary kind, which the guidebook said would respond to antibiotics.

I remembered the doxycycline pills from my doctor at Peoples Clinic in Chicago. We started taking these, and vomiting them up, and taking more. Within a day, our symptoms had eased enough for us to get downstairs. The hotel guy went and found a taxi to take us to the hospital. The ride through potholed streets was intolerable, but neither of us threw up. We arrived at the hospital—and it was closed. A sign said the place was open Tuesday and Thursday, from nine AM to one PM. Today was Wednesday.

The taxi took us back.

We spent another week recuperating under the beneficent influence of the doxycycline. Then, we moved to a nicer hotel, on the shore of Phewa Lake, the center of trekkers' life in Pokhara.

We'd settled into our new room, and were out for a walk, when a girl approached. "Would you like a mushroom omelet?"

Chris asked, "What kind of mushrooms?"

"Magic mushrooms. I collect them by the road. I can get you some in a few minutes." She prepared the omelet and we ate it half an hour later.

We went down to the lakeside and rented a rowboat. As the mushrooms started to alter us, we rowed to the center of the lake.

Rising all around were stepped green hillsides, intensely cultivated. Beyond were more hills: a fairy-tale landscape that rose and repeated. In the high distance were the Himalayas. From studying the trekking books, I knew the identities of several mountains by their shapes: Dhaulagiri, Machhapuchhare, Annapurna.

From the peak of Annapurna, thirty miles distant, I could see snow billowing sideways. This must have been a miles-long blizzard, but it looked clean, stable, and eternal.

I realized that this moment on Phewa Lake, gazing at the snow blowing off Annapurna, would always remain my life's exact center.

We found a used bookstore, in a trailer, run by a guy from New Zealand. I bought a copy of *The Two Towers*. Stoned on hash, I couldn't stop reading; I kept repeating the same page over and over.

Two days later, we headed into the mountains. There were lots of foreigners climbing the paths. Many had local porters; we carried our own packs. For once, I'd left my sax behind, and I missed it. But—it was difficult going up and up.

We slept in hostels. The views were pure Middle Earth. The mountains got closer. We'd walk for three hours along a dry streambed with the gigantic diamond shape of Machhapuchhare in front the whole time, then turn upward into a jungle with monkeys screaming from the trees.

We got to the top of Poon Hill, three days from Pokhara—ten thousand feet up—and decided to turn back. It was cold; there was snow; we didn't have the right clothes. We hadn't prepared for more than six days up and down.

Two days later, heading down a narrow, gravelly path in twilight, Chris slipped and hurt her ankle. She limped for an hour until we got to the hostel at Ghorepani.

We bound her ankle the next morning: she would have to walk on it. By late afternoon, we could see Phewa Lake in the distance, but we knew the path would take us around by a longer, indirect route through the town of Pokhara itself. We decided to try head straight down, to arrive at the lake from the near side. After sliding down a series of terraces, we found ourselves trapped in a labyrinth of rice paddies broken into rectangular pools with baulks bounding them. We had to walk carefully on these narrow, raised bridges of earth so as not to slip into the pools. Because our packs were heavy, though, we did keep slipping, damaging the baulks. Somehow, we kept going—we had no choice.

After an hour, we came out onto a road that led around to the hotels on Phewa Lake.

We took a bus south, crossed into India near Gorakhpur, and caught a train to Varanasi. We stayed at a hotel by the burning ghats. In the morning, a boatman took us out on the Ganges. As we watched corpses being burned while pilgrims waded into the river, another boat paddled up and the flute-seller on board let me try some out. I bought two.

We walked in the marketplace, and down to Banaras Hindu University, where Krishnamurti was scheduled to speak in a few days. We weren't prepared to stick around, though, and instead caught a train to Delhi.

When we checked at the American Express office for mail, the woman told me there was a message from the American Embassy. I should go there immediately.

I'd sent the assistant state's attorney American Express office addresses in Japan and India, and I suspected this message was from him. I was right: at the embassy, they told me to telephone Chicago, as the trial for the killing I'd witnessed was about to begin. I asked if I could use their phone, and they were dismissive: I should go to an international telephone exchange. They gave me an address for one near our hotel in Connaught Circle.

I had to call in the middle of the night because it would be daytime in Chicago. We waited till one AM, then made our way to the exchange. There was a line extending out the door. The guy at the embassy had warned us about these lines and suggested a strategy for jumping to the front. All I had to say was, "It's about a murder!" I did this—trying to sound dramatic—and we were promptly sitting in a booth, while an operator in another room dialed the number.

The call went through and after a little confusion the assistant state's attorney—his voice faint—was saying, "You've got to come back. You'll be testifying in ten days."

I complained. We'd been planning to visit Sri Lanka. It would be inconvenient and expensive to return to Chicago right away.

"Don't worry about that. We'll pay for your plane ticket." His voice was fading.

"So, you'll pay for my ticket? How will you buy it?"

"You buy your ticket, we'll pay you back."

We took a train to Agra and visited the Taj Mahal. I got out my sax and spent an hour in the garden playing long tones. We caught a bus to Ajanta and roamed the caves, taking in the fifth-century murals as around our heads swooped squeaking bats. In the glare of our guide's flashlight, the faded colors depicted lush Gupta court life: princes with ineffable expressions; dancing courtesans.

We went to Ellora and spent a day in the Deccan hills among stone gods in networks of hermits' caves carved hundreds of feet into volcanic magma. A massive temple had been carved in detail out of black rock.

We spent the night in Aurangabad and took a plane to Bombay. After eighteen hours in the airport, we were suddenly flying away from India. We touched down in Kuwait: desert, nothing but sand—technology! An airport! A little later, we were back in the air. A few hours to London, a change of planes, and eight hours later we were landing at O'Hare. We'd circled the globe.

It was freezing. We caught a limo to Evanston and spent the night with Chris' former assistant manager, Connie Reuveuni.

We'd hit Chicago two days before my scheduled trial appearance. Just when we'd left India, we'd seen in the paper that dozens of police officers had attacked a village of Dalits. They'd gouged out the eyes of hundreds of villagers, then killed them.

Chicago, with its paltry three-cops-one-victim brutality, sure seemed mild by comparison.

In India, we'd become accustomed to the sight of abject misery: people without arms and legs rolling on wheeled boards, begging in the streets.

In Chicago, I listened to the radio as a woman complained about the gas company cutting off heat when she couldn't pay her bill. I saw homeless men who had coats and shoes.

The culture shock was just so intense, coming straight back. I couldn't figure out where I was and what I should think. Man, was America rich! In India, people picked up cow-turds and slapped them on walls to dry, for later use as fuel. No piece of trash was too small for salvage by some specialist. America was the land of excess and the home of waste.

The morning of my testimony, Chris and I went down to the courthouse at 26th and California. There were a couple dozen anti-police-brutality protesters chanting out front—

Reverend Jesse Jackson was involved. Chris was allowed into the courtroom to sit with other spectators; I was sent to a waiting room.

When I was called to the witness box, I saw those cops from the 35th Street station sitting at the desk diagonally across from me. I was able to verify for myself that they had in fact been the same men who'd tried to intimidate me, on Clarendon.

They didn't meet my stare.

I knew ten eyewitnesses had materialized: the prosecution had a strong case. I told my story. During cross-examination, the defense attorney tried to get me to say something confusing about where the Black man's arms had been when the big guy was sitting on him, but I didn't change my words, and he gave up. I spent only a few minutes on the stand.

Chris told me afterward that just before me a police officer had testified. A week after the beating he'd given a statement that implicated the cops I'd seen. Today on the witness stand he'd recanted, saying he'd been mistaken.

The story that emerged from the trial was that the Black guy was Richard Ramey, who'd been kicked out of a mental institution six months earlier, due to a cut-off of state funds. Since there was no-one to take care of him, he'd been wandering the city. The two white men, Fred Earullo and Louis Klisz (the huge one)—along with the other guy in street-clothes who I'd seen come in with the uniformed officers, Fred Christiano—were undercover transit cops. That's why they hadn't had uniforms. Their job was to roam El trains looking for trouble.

Richard Ramey had been smoking a cigarette on the El. The undercover cops had told him to stop, and he'd refused. When they'd tried to take the cigarette from him, Ramey had supposedly stabbed one with a pen. This had enraged them enough to give Ramey the five-hour beating that killed him.

The witnesses' testimony said the cops had started hitting Ramey on the train, then taken him down the steps into the 35th Street station, where I'd seen them. Then, they'd put him in a squad car, where the beating had continued. Then, he'd been beaten in the front room of the stationhouse. Finally, in a holding pen, the beating had gone on.

The cops had reported he'd died of a heart attack, and his injuries were self-inflicted: incurred resisting arrest.

The eyewitnesses persuaded the judge. My own actions had generated electronic evidence: an audiotape of me narrating the crime to the nine-one-one operator.

Judge Cieslik convicted Earullo and Klisz of involuntary manslaughter and a few months later sentenced them to a couple of years in jail. Not much—considering what they'd done—but more than anyone expected. Jesse Jackson commented to the press, "This verdict does not meet the truest ends of justice, for Mr. Ramey was murdered. The only surprise in the ruling was that they were not exonerated absolutely. [The ruling is] a blanket endorsement for the police to engage in open-season abuse and killing of black and brown males."

Still—it had been worth coming back from India.

The court did not reimburse my plane ticket. The assistant state's attorney changed his mind because before the trial he'd phoned my mother, and during their conversation, she'd mentioned the postcard I'd sent two months earlier saying we might return to the US by Christmas.

Thanks, Mom.

I learned the full tale decades later, when author Rebecca Migdal was researching the trial for a graphic novel. She showed me Robert Cooley's memoir, *When Corruption Was King: How I Helped the Mob Rule Chicago, Then Brought the Outfit Down,* in which I read, "An important part of the story never made it into the press. One of the cops was related to Angelo LaPietra, the little king of the Chinatown group, and Hook wanted to make sure the case was fixed."

The cops had requested a bench trial because a pliant judge could be lined up: unlike with a jury trial, acquittal could be guaranteed. Judge Arthur Cieslik, however, had felt unexpected qualms because of the horror of the crime and the plethora of evidence. In sentencing the cops to prison, Cieslik had defied his mob patrons.

Judge Cieslik's upright conduct during the Ramey trial had an afterlife. Although he was a longtime mob lawyer and fixer, Robert Cooley took inspiration:

> I watched a few hours of testimony. Witness after witness got up to describe the way the two cops mercilessly beat the victim while he was in handcuffs. … During the sentencing hearing, I continued to see the judge each day after court. He would say, "I just can't give them probation for this type of crime." I would simply say, "Just do what you think is right." He wound up sentencing the cops to time. … Cieslik really did do

the right thing, and by providing him some moral support, I may have helped. I liked the way that felt. Now, more than ever, I questioned the life I had made for myself as a lawyer.

A few years later, Cooley approached the FBI, proposing to wear a wire to produce evidence exposing Chicago's corrupt judicial system. Cooley's dangerous game succeeded: during Operation GambAt, the feds successfully prosecuted dozens of dirty politicians and judges, as well as quite a few of the mobsters running the show.

Rebecca Migdal also found out that Judge Cieslik had paid a price for his independence: he'd been subjected to a smear campaign that ended his judicial career. According to research conducted by his daughter Debra Cieslik—chronicled on her blog—this was mob payback.

No good deed goes unpunished.

5-REFUGEES IN PARIS

JANUARY 1982

We flew to Paris a few weeks after my testimony—relieved to get out of reach of retaliation—but a snowstorm forced our plane down in Brussels, so we arrived in Paris by train, receiving no French visa-stamps in our passports, a dubious beginning.

Our first night, an Iranian man approached us in the hotel lobby pleading for help getting a new American visa. In perfect English he said he'd gone to college in Ohio, then become a pilot in the Shah's private air-force. He was jailed by the mullahs after the revolution in '79. Two weeks ago, his relatives had managed to bribe some prison guards to leave his cell door unlocked. The relatives had smuggled him a plane ticket from Pakistan to New York via Paris, as well as his pre-revolution passport, in which were stamped a French visa and an American visa he'd obtained as a precaution before the Shah's overthrow.

After fleeing jail, he'd walked for days across a desert into Pakistan. He'd flown to Paris where, to his shock, immigration had just rejected his French visa as expired, and pointed out that he wouldn't be able to use the old American visa either. He'd been allowed into town for forty-eight hours to try and solve his problem. He couldn't speak French.

I suggested he might qualify as a political refugee, so he should go to the office of the United Nations High Commissioner for Refugees. He said he didn't know how. Would we take him? I looked in the phone book, and there was in fact an office of the UNHCR in Paris. The next day—our second in Paris—Chris and I went with the Iranian to the UNHCR. We sat in the waiting room while he left with a refugee officer to discuss his situation.

A fellow sitting next to us introduced himself as an activist from Cairo, working for democracy in Egypt. When we said we were from Chicago, he said, "I didn't know there were refugees from America."

I smiled but caught myself in time not to recount my police brutality tale. You'd better develop self-censorship instincts as an American abroad: his story would likely refer to my tax dollars paying the salaries of brutal police in Egypt.

When the Iranian pilot returned from his conversation, he seemed happier. Chris and I switched to a cheaper hotel the next day and lost track of him, with relief. Four hotel moves later, we finally came up with an apartment in the Ninth Arrondissement.

It took us a few weeks of querying and research to figure out our business idea wouldn't work. To launch a newsstand as American citizens, we'd need a French partner who'd own fifty-one percent of the business, and we didn't have any French friends. Plus, our language skills were lousy. Back in Konorak, my high-school French had seemed likely to be adequate to our needs. Not so. We signed up for French classes at an adult education center. For the time being, we were not headed into business, but an American who was also studying French—Lindsay McGowan—helped Chris land a job cooking for an American sculptor who was creating a public monument in the western suburbs.

A Laotian emigre, Charlie Soupanaminth, struck up a conversation with me in Metro Chatelet, where I was making money as a street musician playing shakuhachi. Charlie introduced me to his friend Kong Tong, a Laotian singer with Chinese and Vietnamese restaurant bands. This led to some pick-up gigs, such as playing tenor sax in the back-up band for a vivacious Hong Kong singer whose outfit was mostly feathers.

Charlie also introduced us to a Chinese woman named Elizabeth who hired Chris for private English lessons and invited me to play shakuhachi in her Montparnasse restaurant. Every Saturday night, I'd set up a music stand just inside the front door and play Kinko songs, then go table to table with a plate to collect tips. One night a man said (in French) that he hadn't liked it.

"You didn't like the music?"

"I didn't like the musician."

I continued to collect from other tables. After I left, a woman rushed out and handed me fifty francs. "That man was rude. Your music was nice and so were you."

On bulletin boards in music stores I posted announcements saying I'd studied with the AACM in Chicago and Soke Chikayu-sha in Tokyo, and was offering lessons in jazz saxophone, flute, chromatic harmonica and shakuhachi. Within a few weeks, I had students coming by our apartment. One afternoon, during an energetic free-jazz lesson, a woman screamed across the rooftops, *"C'est la merde! C'est la merde!"*

By June, Kong Tong had helped me land a five-hours-a-night, seven-nights-a-week job playing flute, tenor sax, and chromatic harmonica with a five-piece band in a huge Chinese restaurant with a dance floor, called Mandarin du Forum—on the lowest level of the underground Forum des Halles mall, in the middle of town. Over the next five months, I developed a repertoire of Taiwanese pop tunes and Hong Kong movie themes. An especially proud moment was when Douglas Ewart—with whom I'd kept in touch by mail—took an hour out of his European concert tour to come by and chat.

Each night at two AM, the band would let me sing. I'd pick up the microphone and launch into "One Meatball" or "House of the Rising Sun," always doing my honest best—but inevitably straggling diners would look up in shock, pay their bills and get out.

Kong Tong sang with the group for an hour most nights. He worked in five different languages. Performing "Paloma," he'd wail in falsetto while I harmonized up in the altissimo register of my tenor sax. Another Laotian singer, who called himself Johnny—people told him he looked like Johnny Mathis—liked to perform the Frank Sinatra tune "My Way." Unrepentant big-man deathbed anthem purveyed by six music nerds.

I was welcomed into this circle of Asian musicians because I was an American who'd lived in Asia, and they were refugees and emigres from Southeast Asia, who'd been friends with Americans during the Vietnam War, a decade before. One night, Chang the piano player, who'd played music for American soldiers in Saigon nightclubs, drew a map of Vietnam on a napkin. "Here's the South; here's the North; here's the DMZ. Why did you Americans stay south of the DMZ?" He drew a series of arrows on the napkin. "You should just invade the North!"

Another time, one of the restaurant's owners approached me unexpectedly and said, "I was at the embassy in Saigon the day you Americans left. You took off in your helicopters from the roof. You didn't care. You left us all behind." I kept myself from blurting out, "Hey, it wasn't me!" or, "I supported the American pullout." Instead I said, "I'm so sorry."

We caught soprano-sax legend Steve Lacy with composer/pianist Frederic Rzewski at American Center for Art and Culture. Lacy was one of my heroes; twenty years earlier he'd played with the fabulous Thelonious Monk and now he was the frequent partner of my favorite pianist, Mal Waldron, who I knew lived in Munich. After the final applause, I darted out of my seat, up the aisle, onto the stage, and asked for a lesson.

Steve Lacy looked startled, and replied, "Gee, man, I don't teach."

I retreated. Damn; too eager.

Months too late for me, I heard that with Steve Lacy, you could just show up at his house and hang around.

* * *

After civil-rights icon Nina Simone's concert at Le Chat Qui Peche—"Mississippi Goddamn" and "Sinnerman" soaring over thunderous piano—Nina asked the audience if anyone who could speak English and French would accompany her to the headquarters of SACEM, which manages musical copyright in Europe. Simone was trying to regain control of her pirated work.

I knew Nina Simone had left the US years before, to escape racism. Apparently, she was being exploited here as well. I raised my hand—but when I introduced myself, she was uneasy. She probably wouldn't be able to use my help.

Chris and I found ourselves chatting with a woman who'd already been advising Nina. Margot Bostrom whispered that Andy was the name of Nina Simone's abusive ex-husband.

Margot was a New Yorker doing computer consulting and trying to build a career as a songwriter. She'd been a teen speedfreak in the fifties and used to hang out at Birdland when bebop was hot. We got together with her regularly over the next few months, including at a fortieth birthday party she threw for Noah Howard, the free-jazz saxophonist from New Orleans. Like Nina Simone, he'd left to escape racism—actually, there was an entire diaspora of American jazz refugees in Europe.

Margot introduced Chris to an Egyptian named Sion, who was running an English school for kindergarteners. Chris taught there till she was nearly insane. Fortunately, another teaching job at a place called Stein and Company materialized, and Chris was able to leave kindergarten.

* * *

I finally got the chance to meet my idol George Lewis after his concert with English free-improv guitarist Derek Bailey, at Rue Dunois. There was no trombone: George had gotten into computer sounds—though he did blow squeaks on a drinking straw he snipped short with scissors. When I told him about my move to Chicago in '79, he explained that he'd left for New York in '78, but Douglas Ewart was his longtime collaborator.

I started taking lessons in harmony and composition with Steve Carbonara, an American who'd recently graduated from the Berklee College of Music in Boston. Steve had just set up a school called The American Academy of Modern Music. Through him, I met several American musicians including Jeff Beer, a trumpet player from Chicago. Jeff was in Celestrial Communication Orchestra (CCO), directed by Alan Silva, who'd played bass and violin in the sixties with pianist Cecil Taylor and dozens of other free-jazz pioneers, leaving New York a few years later for Paris. CCO operated out of Alan's school for improvising musicians called Institut Art Culture Perception. At Jeff's suggestion, I started taking group improv lessons at Institut Art Culture Perception, in hopes I'd be invited to join CCO.

My classmates and I constituted a band: drums, bass, guitar, tenor sax, alto sax (me), cello, trumpet, and trombone. Plus, Alan Silva himself, sometimes shouting instructions and commentary, sometimes commandeering the drum set and turning the music around, sometimes listening intensely, with his lanky body hunched over his knees, hands cradling his knit-cap-covered head, eyes scrunched shut.

Alan specialized in the Schillinger technique of composition, as adapted by Cecil Taylor to the art of improvisation. We would generate counter-intuitive melodic lines using elaborate techniques. We might take a standard jazz tune, write out the melody upside down or backwards, multiply or divide the rhythms into halves or thirds or sixths, transpose the melody up a fourth or down a third, and then intersplice the versions together, note by note, to create a new super-complicated version. Then we'd subject this super-version to its own round of the procedures, generating a hyper-super-version. We'd each tackle these tasks independently and come up with unique results. Having written out our strange constructions, we'd improvise simultaneously, using as our melodic materials chunks and fragments of these hard-to-play lines. You could hear the original tune deep in the startling structure of our joint sound.

One purpose of this exercise was to break us of old habits and force us to do new things. I'd never realized how many personal clichés I'd developed. It was amazing to hear myself playing sounds I'd never heard before. Alan admonished us, on the subject of mastering your instrument, "Why would anyone ever want to do anything less than perfect?!"

Alan didn't speak too much French—as far as I could tell—and I was the only American in our class. His English was unusual too, including compound words he seemed to make up on the spot which nevertheless, I could understand. He sounded like a beat poet: early ecstatic Allen Ginsberg.

I became Alan Silva's translator during those months, though he never asked me to. The other students looked so bewildered when he launched into his jazzy, hyper-poetic English that I couldn't keep quiet. He'd talk for a minute, then stop, and I'd do a thirty-second translation while he looked at me with a worried expression. When I finished, he'd talk for another minute, and I'd translate some more. I have no clue whether my translations carried specific meaning, but I remember people nodding their heads in comprehension. After all, many of Alan's elaborations on the essence of what we were doing didn't have specific meaning in English. I'd say, *"C'est a dire"* (That's to say), or *"Ce qu'il dit"* (What he's saying), and then take off with my own made-up French, full of cognates of Alan's locutions and guesses at his philosophical theories. Pure expressionism. I never spoke better French.

Meanwhile, I figured out that my invitation to join Celestrial Communication Orchestra wasn't imminent: they had a full complement of saxophonists.

I answered an ad on a notice board: a singer named Dorian was looking for a sax player to accompany cabaret songs. Dorian turned out to be the stage name of Rob Grayson, who'd worked for Chris at Dalton's before my time. We'd met: he'd once dropped by, dressed in singing-telegram uniform.

Dorian was in Paris trying to break through, specializing in stylish renditions of tunes like "Johnny One Note," "Satin Doll," and "New York, New York." I dragged in a piano player named Eddie who I'd met through Steve Carbonara and we played a hilarious trio gig at a salon for aspiring poets and artists, hosted in an ostentatious apartment by some Australians who'd gotten rich in the trucking business.

I was also half of a flute-and-guitar duo with Bruce McVicker. We'd slide into a crowded restaurant on Rue Mouffetard, improvise on "Autumn Leaves" and "One Note Samba" for ten minutes, move among tables collecting tips, then zip over to the restaurant next door and play some more.

The trio and duo each gave a performance at Galerie Robinson: my own shows, in Paris! Well—not my compositions—not creative music.

As in Japan, it was fun—for a while. Chris cooked and taught during the day while I took classes. I played restaurant music seven nights a week. We didn't see much of each other.

It became a grind. We'd moved to Paris to get out of Chicago and open our own store. Paris was beautiful but this life wasn't what we'd planned: opening a legit business probably wasn't in the cards, since we'd been working illegally, had almost no French friends, and had overstayed our permitted three-month tourist visit (although—with no entry stamps in our passports, this could not be proved against us). In August, at the height of the tourist season, having grabbed a little time together in the afternoon, we were jostling in a huge crowd on the Left Bank when we heard one American tourist say to another, "Wouldn't you just die to live here?" We looked at each other and rolled our eyes.

By November, our routine was getting really old. We weren't bona fide refugees. True, Earullo and Klisz were still at large—they'd appealed—but we knew if we wanted to open our bookstore, we should brave their threat and return to Chicago, where Chris' professional contacts could open doors.

On our last day in Paris, a guy from the rental agency showed up minutes before we left for the airport. I had a full pack on my back and Chris was downstairs, when he blocked me in the apartment and demanded I leave a couple hundred dollars in case we'd made long-distance calls.

We hadn't made any, but he didn't believe me. I tried to push past, but he jumped, and wrestled me to the floor, yelling, *"Vous etes Americain, mais vous etes un homme quand meme!"* Chris snuck up and grabbed his papers, then threatened to burn them with a lighter. This freaked him out and we ended up doing a paperwork-for-Andy swap—then cramming into our friends' car and hightailing it.

The agent's exclamation translates as, "You're American, but you're still a man," however I'd say his meaning was more the classic insult, "You think you're hot shit in a champagne glass, but you're really cold diarrhea in a dixie cup."

6-RETURNING THE FAVOR

DECEMBER 1982

Jeff Beer had gotten back to Chicago before us. I gave him a call and he said there were amazing jam sessions, Sunday nights, at a new place operated by Stuart Rosenberg called The Space, near the Davis El stop in Evanston. I brought my alto sax, flute, and shakuhachi, and sat in on several tunes.

The pianist was Howard Levy, a musician I'd heard of as a brilliant jazz harmonica player. Since I played jazz—rather poorly—on chromatic harmonica, I was amazed that Howard had developed his own overblowing techniques to play fast, harmonically complex bebop on an ordinary blues harp.

Not only was Howard full of innovative ideas, he was friendly and unassuming. He would comp and stay out of the way of a soloist as happily as get out front.

Howard was enthusiastic about my free-jazz shakuhachi playing. (I felt guilty but knew Kawase Junsuke wouldn't find out that I'd broken my promise.) Howard's mother had given him a shakuhachi and I showed him some of the Japanese head and lip positions.

Jeff Beer introduced me to friends from his days at University of Illinois at Champaign. I'd avoided the North Side jazz venues my previous year in town, not wanting to enter the white Chicago mainstream, but instead be a creative music player with the AACM. Now, I learned that the North Side scene was vibrant, and the Champaign musicians from the seventies were its mainstays. These guys were talented and disciplined. They placed stress on mastering all styles from the history of jazz, something I'd never attempted, since I wasn't deeply attracted to anything but creative music and free jazz.

However, some of these North Side musicians loved free jazz, too. I started jamming weekly with conga-player/performance-artist Robert Metrick, and also with the bassist from those Space sessions, Dan DeLorenzo.

I wanted to renew my involvement with the AACM. In January, I visited Douglas Ewart. His front hallway was almost impassable: jammed with huge pieces of bamboo from Jamaica. Douglas had been transforming these into hochikus, a kind of giant shakuhachi. A samurai spy could do serious damage with these things.

Douglas played, producing impossibly low tones. I tried but couldn't cover the wide lip-opening.

Douglas had originally come as a teen from Jamaica. A Jamaican friend was visiting. The two were listening to a ska record, and I found myself chatting with Janis Lane-Ewart, AACM's administrative director. Janis suggested I sign up for AACM School.

The news there really was an AACM School was a shock.

Back at Yale, I'd heard a rumor of such a place, but in Chicago in '79 and '80, even though I'd attended AACM concerts and met AACM musicians, no-one had mentioned this school.

Janis was surprised to hear it. The school was held every Saturday, in a church at the corner of 74th and Jeffrey, in the South Shore neighborhood. Sign-up for the next term was in one week.

It took an hour-and-a-half by train and bus to get from our apartment in Lakeview down to South Shore. I found myself registering among sixty people, aged five to seventy-five. There were group lessons in all instruments, with private lessons available too. Other subjects included jazz orchestration and jazz history. There was a chorus, a small ensemble, and a large ensemble.

I had no expectations for the school's fee and was nonplussed to find that, after I'd worked out my schedule and completed my form, I was to pay ten dollars for the ten-week quarter.

This seemed like a mistake. Perhaps it was ten dollars per class, per week?

No. It didn't matter how many classes I took during the ten weeks—my cost would be ten dollars.

This school had as its teachers AACM musicians living in Chicago, such as Yosef Ben-Israel, Mwata Bowden, Turk Burton, Kahil El'Zabar, Douglas Ewart, Vandy Harris, Reggie Nicholson, Rita Warford, and Ed Wilkerson, and, as visiting instructors, AACM members who had moved elsewhere, including (while I was there), Roscoe Mitchell, Leo Smith, and Joseph Jarman—and also their friends, such as James Newton.

I was embarrassed to pay ten dollars. The fee was aimed at neighborhood children and community members. I asked to pay one hundred, which Janis Lane-Ewart allowed me to do.

My orchestration class was taught by Vandy Harris, and I was the only student. He had me buy *The Technique of Orchestration,* a standard text. Over the course of ten weeks, Vandy guided me through a slew of exercises, culminating in me transforming a jazz tune that I'd written to a lyric by my friend Laura Kelsey into a full-blown, sixteen-part big-band arrangement.

When George Lewis came through, he gave a group lesson. One student was to sit at the piano while another, through the second-story window, watched traffic. George called out the names of notes and asked students to assign each a color. George requested the kid at the window call each passing car's color; the student at the piano was to play that color's note. As car-colors were called, the traffic's melody played.

Large Ensemble was directed by Mwata Bowden, a clarinet and saxophone master. Mwata guided us thirty students in playing a variety of unusual compositions and structured improvisations designed by AACM members. The camaraderie among children, teens, and adults of all ages was wonderful, as we interpreted sheet music covered with rhythmic symbols, maze-like squiggles, and bursts of musical notation, amid shifting time-signatures.

I struck up an acquaintance with the other tenor-sax players. Floyd Webb was the founder of Blacklight Film Festival. Nancy Hazelton—the other white student—was a nurse. One afternoon, Nancy gave me a ride downtown. I was telling her about the Richard Ramey murder.

"You saw that? I was at Cook County that year. I was doing paperwork when I came across the x-rays of Ramey's body: the same doctors had examined him. His ribs were all broken, contusions and bruises so severe. A bunch of us nurses passed those x-rays around. The cops had worked him over everywhere. Did you know that was a five-hour beating? I've never seen a body so messed up. And they claimed he died of a heart attack!"

"I should have hung around in the El station. Maybe they'd have stopped hitting him."

"Are you kidding? They'd have beaten you, too."

Meanwhile, Robert Metrick had invited me to play bass clarinet during his "Elusive Cha-Cha" show at Crosscurrents, alongside Jeff Beer on trumpet. We accompanied Lynn Book as she vocalized Robert's deadpan rap: "My face fell on the sidewalk / I ran to call the doctor / He came and looked so jealous." A month later, Stuart Rosenberg booked Dan DeLorenzo and me for a duo show at The Space, playing structured-improv compositions we'd developed—creative music *a la* AACM—including my wacky arrangement for Gertrude Stein's poem "Ladies Voices." With all this North-Side jamming and performance, I began to sense my musical career emerging.

Attrition is a problem for small independent schools. One Saturday, when only five of us had come for AACM School Large Ensemble, Mwata gave a pep talk: "If the trumpet player doesn't show up, what do you do? You hit! If the trumpet player and the saxophone player don't show up, what do you do? You hit! If the trumpet player and the saxophone player and the drummer don't show up, what do you do? You hit! If the trumpet and saxophone and drums and bass don't show up, what do you do! You hit! If only you show up, what do you do? You hit!"

I signed up for three successive ten-week quarters at AACM School. During the hottest days of summer, for three Saturdays, I was the only student who showed up for Large Ensemble. Mwata and I played hour-long duo improvisations: him on bari sax, me on bass clarinet; him on alto, me on flute; him on clarinet, me on kalimba. We hit!

Another course had a different impact on me and demanded a different response. This was jazz history with percussionist Turk Burton. I knew a lot about jazz history—self-taught, plus, at Yale I'd taken a class with composition professor Robert Morris—but Turk's emphasis was political.

Jazz history, like the history of all Black cultural contribution, is a story about Black people creating and white people benefiting financially. If you think this is a stereotype or an over-simplification, it's not.

Just as my gut response to the Mandarin du Forum owner's complaint about the American desertion of South Vietnam was, "Hey, it wasn't me," I'd always felt that I, as a young white musician, was different from old white musicians. I hadn't been involved in the white theft of Black music, because I hadn't been there. But Turk Burton's thorough, even-tempered, weeks-long elucidation of the Black-to-white trail from Buddy Bolden to Bix Beiderbecke, then from Fletcher Henderson to Benny Goodman, then from Duke Ellington to Glen Miller, then from Lester Young to Stan Getz, finally started to hit home.

I realized that…I might be some sort of success—on the North Side.

I'd have no trouble showing up on time for gigs. I'd talk pleasantly to club owners and people with money to make records. I'd be friendly with audiences. I'd very likely—at least subconsciously—tweak my music to please listeners. I could communicate in several languages.

I had access to my family's financial support.

I was white. That alone would open doors which those door-openers would heatedly deny were closed to Black musicians.

Where did this leave me, ethically?

Sure, I knew of many white jazz players—like Steve Lacy—who'd chosen to live in sync with the standards set by Black musicians. The decision I made, in August of '83, to respond actively to the white theft of Black music, was not a criticism of any white musician's integrity. Everyone looks in their own mirror. I shared my decision with none of my musician friends.

This was me. I couldn't do it. I wasn't destined to become a white professional musician playing Great Black Music on the North Side.

I'd entered into a delusion I hadn't properly explored. Moving to Chicago to become part of the AACM, I'd overlooked the uncertainty principle: the observer alters the thing observed. I did become part of the AACM scene, and that scene, with me in it, was different. There was something not quite right about the way I'd plunked myself there.

The AACM on the South Side of Chicago was the wellspring, the root. In the tradition. Everyone in Paris had thought of me as a Chicago musician who'd studied with the AACM. Yes, that was my history. But it contained a lie, because Great Black Music wasn't my tradition.

Turk Burton did not suggest I stop playing. I jammed with him in Large Ensemble. All the AACM musicians were welcoming; exceedingly generous. I simply came to realize that their generosity demanded reciprocal respect.

When a person creates something, and another person sees it, and decides they want to do the same thing, this second person has not done what the first person did. Imitating and extending are different than innovating.

If the second person can also foresee he may receive acclaim and financial benefit, using the thing the first person created—and, perhaps, he will get more acclaim and more financial benefit than that first person ever did—then the second person cannot ignore that he has made a decision.

And if you tie in hundreds of years of slavery and Jim-Crow abuse with present-day racism and police brutality—that's where the white theft of Black music comes in.

Music is not property, it's a gift freely shared. But musicians are people who need and deserve acknowledgment and remuneration. So many marvelous white musicians had successfully adapted the innovations of the Black musicians, and became popular, and made a living, while the brilliant originators were poorly paid, or went to prison, or spent horrible years in the army, or died young, and then, lots of those white musicians took the success and higher earnings as their due. De facto cultural theft from Black musicians.

THE MUSIC THIEF

I was not prepared to become a music thief. The only honest way I should make this music I loved was now and then—on the side.

It's not too much to say that few white people in America go to any effort to figure out that you can't be white unless there's someone who's Black, so every white American is implicated in the history of the oppression of Black Americans.

As with my struggle around being middle class, when it came to the white theft of Black music, I wasn't so dumb as to wallow in guilt. I only needed to find my direct action. You didn't always get the chance to fix a past mistake. But sometimes you did, and it felt great to come to a realization, and make that choice. Abandoning my plan to play creative music professionally gave me the opportunity to seek a vocation truer to myself. A week before my last class at AACM School, I was hired by Victor and June Podagrosi of Child's Play Touring Theatre to be a full-time actor, performing stories and poems written by children. Over the next two years, I worked in hundreds of schools

Meanwhile, on the side, I played a few gigs with Jeff Beer's Ancient Babies quintet, then convened Paradox Opera with Jeff Beer, Lynn Book, Dan DeLorenzo, Phil Helzer, Johnse Holt, Dot Kane and Doug Smith. We mounted three multimedia nights at Chicago Filmmakers with production by Robert Metrick: two performances of the Dada-themed *Evening of the Bearded Heart,* featuring Kurt Schwitters' *Sonata in Primeval Sounds,* then an evening called *Amerika: Chaplin/Kafka/Stein/Mayakovsky*—a collage of dialogues, films and songs about feeling foreign in America.

Finally, in September of '85, Chris and I fulfilled our dream, opening The Children's Bookstore, with "the largest, best selection of children's books in the Chicago area" (according to *Chicago Tribune*), plus tons of free programs for families. And we loved booking AACM shows for kids: Ed Wilkerson and Rita Warford, Douglas Ewart and Inventions, the AACM School Small Ensemble. Our first year, we won the Women's National Book Association's Pannell Award for being the booksellers who'd done the most to bring children and books together.

My calling was bookselling.

Douglas Ewart guides the AACM School Small Ensemble, in a 1986 performance at The Children's Bookstore. Photo: Ed Sacks.

POSTSCRIPT

A few months after we returned from Paris, those cops lost their appeal and went to prison. Once they'd served their brief sentences—and until Chris and I moved to Amherst in 2002—we shared Chicago with them.

As owner of The Children's Bookstore, I was a public figure; my name was sometimes in the newspaper or on the radio. For years, the bookstore received anonymous, threatening letters: sometimes clustered together, sometimes a year apart. They were always two pages long, hand typed, and filled with vitriol and horrible intent. Without proof, I figured they were from Fred Earullo. Prison is a great place to vow revenge.

As Jesse Jackson said, what Fred Earullo and Louis Klisz did to Richard Ramey was not manslaughter; it was murder. By the lights of the justice system they worked for, those bastards should have spent decades behind bars. Instead, thanks to racism, they lived free among family and friends.

They're dead, now (of natural causes): Klisz, in 2008; Earullo, in March 2020.

Police brutality lives on.

*   *   *

THE MUSIC THIEF

In '96 I was summoned to jury duty. In the courtroom, a couple dozen prospective jurors were asked to raise their hands if unable to serve for any of several enumerated reasons: health issues, personal economic hardship, hearing disorder, or—to my surprise—"Do you have any reason to disbelieve the sworn testimony of a police officer?"

I raised my hand.

"What is your concern?"

"I was a witness in the Richard Ramey police brutality case."

The prosecutor conferred briefly with his team, then asked, "For the defense?"

I had to consider. "No, for the prosecution."

He shared a glance with the judge, then barked, "Get him outa here!" The bailiff waved energetically, I squeezed down the aisle past my fellow citizens. Evidently, I'd located a legitimate loophole to avoid jury duty.

Decades later, in February 2020, I found myself again in a courtroom—this time, in Easton, Pennsylvania—along with several dozen prospective jurors, as questions were posed about incapacity to serve.

It was number fifteen: "Do you have any reason to disbelieve the sworn testimony of a police officer?" I raised my hand. Ten minutes later, I was seated in an antechamber, facing a stern judge, with the prosecutor to one side, the defense attorney to the other. The judge asked, "What's the problem here?"

"I saw two police officers murder a Black man, in Chicago, in 1980. I testified against them, and they were sent to jail. During the trial, several officers testified falsely under oath."

As I spoke, I realized these people were children back then—maybe, not even born.

The judge drew her eyebrows together sternly. "That was forty years ago."

"Things haven't changed."

"And you're saying it's the same here as in Chicago?"

"To me, the police culture doesn't seem much different."

They stopped wasting time. I was unfit to be a juror.

As I left the courthouse, I wondered: was I merely avoiding jury duty? Should I have kept my mouth shut—that is, lied—so as to be that juror who advocated skepticism of police?

Should questioning authority disqualify jurors?

Coleridge's "willing suspension of disbelief" applies to fiction, not testimony.

ACKNOWLEDGMENTS

Thanks to my musical mentors: Mwata Bowden, Turk Burton, Steve Carbonara, Ned Corman, Douglas Ewart, Vandy Harris, Kawase Junsuke, Van Lemberg, Alan Silva, and John Turner.

Thanks to my professors and teachers: Michael Ferber, Dorothy Fleming, Josephine Forsberg, Rick Hendra, Gary Lazenby, and Robert Morris.

Thanks to my musical acquaintances and performance colleagues: Jeff Beer, Karl Berger, Lynn Book, Raphael D'Lugoff, Dan DeLorenzo, Kahil El'Zabar, David Fertig, Jahmes Finlayson, Dorian Grayson, Nancy Hazelton, Philip Hart Helzer, Junji Hirose, Johnse Holt, Greg Jarby, Howard Levy, George Lewis, Bruce McVicker, Bill Meade, Robert Metrick, Stuart Rosenberg, Ellen Rosner, Ted Sabety, Baker Salsbury, Sooch San Souci, Kate Sanderson, Kong Tong, Rita Warford, Brenda Webb, Floyd Webb, Ed Wilkerson and Morgan Witthoft.

Thanks to my children's theater friends: Todd Bethel, Barbara Chusid, Rachel Feldberg, Dot Kane, Ann Klotz, Kerro Knox, Rhonda Lipkin, Rudolf Munro, June Podagrosi, Victor Podagrosi, Julia Poirier, Kay Saakvitne, Cathy Schuman, Rich Selden, Doug Smith, Debbie Taylor, and Valerie Wattenberg.

Thanks to friends who appear in this book and who offered advice with the manuscript: Mitch Ahern, Paul Berlanga, Margot Bostrom, Wendy Weiss Calkins, Brian Cooper, Michael Edwalds, Mark Elder, Janis Lane Ewart, Ted Fishman, Paul Gulino, Bill Heinrich, Phil Heinrich, Mike Ierardi, Laura Kelsey, Peter Kruley, Maya Lin, Lindsay McGowan, Matt Perry, Connie Reuveni, Charlie Soupanaminth, Vivoo Sugiyama, Loren Warboys, Melissa Wattenberg, Bernie Weiss, and Tom Weiss.

Thanks to the cover artist, Mary Phelan. Thanks to Ed Sacks, The Children's Bookstore's photographer.

Thanks to family members: Christine Bluhm, Claire Laties Davis, Nancy Laties Feresten, Martha Laties, Samuel Laties, Sarah Laties, and Victor Laties.

Thanks to Richard Ramey, described by his neighbors as a "kind and quiet man." I will forever regret my failure to remain longer in that station, instead of continuing on my way.

Finally, endless gratitude to my soulmate, Rebecca Migdal, who has shared her love, dedication, and research skills, encouraging me to fully explore the truth of my life.

NOTES

PROLOGUE—BLACK AND WHITE

Page 3. "We're not fighting a racial fight"
George E. Lewis, *A Power Stronger Than Itself* (Chicago: University of Chicago Press, 2008) 114.

Page 3. "unstable polyphony of quoted voices"
George E. Lewis, *A Power Stronger Than Itself* (Chicago: University of Chicago Press, 2008) 498-501.

1—SIXTIES KID

Page 5. "pictures by Ben Shaun"
Ben Shaun, *Civil Rights Portfolio* (New York: American Civil Liberties Union, 1965). The Freedom Summer murders took place in 1964.

Page 6. "MCPEARL is a Monroe County, New York, coalition working to keep public funds for public schools only. MCPEARL is dedicated to the protection of free public education, open to all children; and committed to the preservation of religious liberty as guaranteed by both eh Federal and state constitutions. … Government support of private schools weakens the public schools. Private schools select their students. They choose the brighter and best-behaved and return children with learning and behavior problems to the public schools. The public schools then must deal with a disproportionate number of children who are difficult to teach and whose presence creates a poorer learning atmosphere for all children. The poorer learning environment then drives able children from public schools to private schools, and the learning environment becomes even worse. Public schools tend to become refuges for the children no private school will accept. Public schools located in poor neighborhoods of big cities have already suffered from this effect."—United States Congress. Senate. Committee on Finance. Subcommittee on Taxation and Debt Management Generally, "Statement of Monroe Citizens for Public Education and Religious Liberty, Martha Laties, Chairman," *Tuition Tax Relief Bills* (Washington, 1978).

Page 6. Leigh Hunt, "Abou Ben Adhem," in *The Book of Gems,* ed. Samuel Carter Hall (London: Saunders and Otley, 1838). Generations of schoolchildren were required to memorize this popular poem. It was loosely inspired by the life of Sufi saint Ibrahim ibn Adham.

My family's Jewish atheism—I learned decades later—was derived from the eighteenth-century Central and Eastern European reform movement called Haskalah: the Jewish Enlightenment.

Page 9. "we were going to learn about discrimination"
"In response to the assassination of Martin Luther King Jr. in 1968, Jane Elliott devised the controversial and startling "Blue Eyes/Brown Eyes Exercise." This now famous, exercise labels participants as inferior or superior based solely upon the color of their eyes and exposes them to the experience of being a minority. Everyone who is exposed to Jane Elliott's work, be it through a lecture, workshop, or video, is dramatically affected by it." Jane Elliott website: http://janeelliott.com.

Page 18. "Victor Gregory Laties, Ph.D. was an important figure in the development of behavioral pharmacology and behavioral toxicology over the final four decades of the 20th century."—University of Rochester website: http://urmc.rochester.edu/libraries/miner/rare-books-and-manuscripts/archives-and-manuscripts/faculty-collections/the-papers-of-victor-g-laties-ph-d.aspx

Page 21. "Ned was back"
Ned Corman, *Now's the Time: A Story of Music, Education, and Advocacy* (Rhinebeck, NY: Epigraph Publishing, 2013).

2—IN AND OUT AT YALE

Page 31. George Lewis, *The George Lewis Solo Trombone Record* (Toronto: Sackville Records, 1977).

Page 34. "they looked cold"
"In 1986, members of Delaware's Native American Nanticoke tribe protested the open display of graves in a sacred site and asked that the facility be closed, out of respect to their ancestors. State officials listened and agreed, and the Island Field museum site is no longer open to the public."—"Island Field site archaeological work in late 1960s," *Cape Gazette,* December 19 2017. http://capegazette.com/article/island-field-site-archaeological-work-late-1960s/148107

Page 39. "pandering to white audiences"
"I always hated the way [Armstrong and Dizzy Gillespie] used to laugh and grin for the audiences. I know why they did it—to make money and because they were entertainers as well as trumpet players. They had families to feed."—Miles Davis, *Miles Davis: The Autobiography*, with Quincey Trope (New York: Simon & Schuster, 1989).

Page 40. Laura Riding, "Autobiography of the Present," *Selected Poems: In Five Sets* (New York: Persea, 1993).

Page 40. Ursula K. Le Guin, *The Dispossessed: An Ambiguous Utopia* (New York: Harper & Row, 1974).

Page 41. Herbert Read, *Anarchy and Order: Essays in Politics* (Boston: Beacon Press, 1971).

3—GOING TO CHICAGO

Page 51. "Christine Bluhm hired me"
Readers of my previous book, *Rebel Bookseller,* will recognize fragments of sentences repeated in this and later chapters. This is because both memoirs—with their different themes—are carved from the same, larger, unpublished manuscript: *Conscience of a Children's Culture Warrior.*
Andrew Laties, *Rebel Bookseller: Why Indie Businesses Represent Everything You Want to Fight For—From Free Speech to Buying Local to Building Communities,* Second Edition ([2005] New York: Seven Stories Press, 2011).

Page 53. Douglas Ewart served as AACM chairman from 1979 to 1986. "Perhaps best known as a composer, improviser, sculptor and maker of masks and instruments, Douglas R. Ewart is also an educator, lecturer, arts organization consultant and all around visionary."—Homepage, http://douglasewart.com

Page 53. "The AACM first coined the phrase Great Black Music to describe its unique direction in music. The AACM pays homage to the diverse styles of expression within the body of Black Music in the USA, Africa and throughout the world. This experience extends from the ancient musics of Africa to the music of the future."—AACM website: http://aacmchicago.org/about

Page 53. "Black and white musicians teaching together"
"Their goal was to establish a nonprofit organization focused on improvisation and musical cross-pollination that complemented musicians' academic studies, a place where music as a universal language could be explored and expanded. They called it the Creative Music Studio. ... Hundreds of Guiding Artists...lived, played and shared musical wisdom with thousands of participants."—http://creativemusic.org/about/history

Page 57. "Kahil El'Zabar"
"El'Zabar began studying African music at an early age, taking a special interest in drumming. At the age of eighteen, he joined Chicago's Association for the Advancement of Creative Musicians, and by 1975 he was chairman of the organization. During the early 1970s, El'Zabar also formed his own musical group, the Ethnic Heritage Ensemble... His musical abilities have allowed him to play with such greats as Stevie Wonder, Paul Simon and Nina Simone."—The History Makers website: https://www.thehistorymakers.org/biography/kahil-elzabar-39

Page 58. Viola Spolin, *Improvisation for the Theater: A Handbook of Teaching and Directing Techniques* ([1963] Chicago, IL: Northwestern University Press, 1999).

Page 58. "Krapp's Last Tape"
"The path from crime to rehabilitation is rarely as inspired as it was for Rick Cluchey, who found his calling as an actor and theater director after hearing Samuel Beckett's *Waiting for Godot* through the bars of his San Quentin prison cell. ... For the next nine years, until his sentence was commuted in 1966, he ran the newly formed San Quentin Drama Workshop, drawing largely on Beckett's work."—"Beckett's prison protégé: the inmate who became a top interpreter of writer's work," *The Guardian,* January 3, 2016.

Page 59. Carla Bley, Paul Haines and Jazz Composer's Orchestra, *Escalator over the Hill* (New York: JCOA Records, 1971).

4—THERE AND BACK AGAIN

Page 72. "Kawase Junsuke III is head of Chikuyu-sha Shakuhachi Guild, the largest individual group of Kinko shakuhachi players in Japan with branches in Europe and the US." –International Shakuhachi Society: http://komuso.com/people/people.pl?person=36

Page 75. "musical warriors of Zen"
"The shakuhachi was used by a particular sect of Zen priests as a weapon-in-disguise after the carrying of samurai swords was outlawed... The priests of the Fuke sect would wander about playing the bamboo flute—a meditative pursuit...but perhaps also a spy's cover, his eyes and face concealed beneath a woven basket, his flute a handy club."—Note by Stuart Leigh, in "The Way of Watazumi," *The Annals of The International Shakuhachi Society, Volume I,* edited by Dan E. Mayers (Wadhurst, UK: The International Shakuhachi Society, 1987) 189.

Page 81. In the 1939 British hit, "We'll Meet Again"—sung by Vera Lynn—a soldier expresses confidence in his safe return from war (or, of going to heaven).

Page 82. "make them face the truth"
"As we turn to leave, we see these walls stretching into the distance, directing us to the Washington Monument, to the left, and the Lincoln Memorial, to the right, thus bringing the Vietnam Memorial into an historical context. We the living are brought to a concrete realization of these deaths. Brought to a sharp awareness of such a loss, it is up to each individual to resolve or come to terms with this loss. For death, is in the end a personal and private matter, and the area contained with this memorial is a quiet place, meant for personal reflection and private reckoning."—Maya Lin, *Maya Lin's Original Proposal,* 1981. http://vvmf.org/About-The-Wall/history-fo-the-vietnam-veterans-memorial/Maya-Lin/

Page 93. Eyewitness testimony, now posted online:
Michael Caldwell testified that he was with his wife Blenda in the concourse area of the station when two white men on either side of a black man came down the stairs toward him. One of the white men was thin with dark hair and the other had long red hair, an earring in his left ear, a bushy red beard, and a moustache. After they passed, he stopped and watched the two white men throw or shove the black man against the wall several times. The man with the beard then held the black man with his back to a cement post, and the thin man kicked him above the knees and below the chest. At that point, he (Caldwell) went to the ticket agent and, after speaking with her, she made a phone call. On his way back toward his wife, he saw the black man's head being held on the floor by the man with the red beard, and he heard the black man yell, "Murder, murder." He did not see any other person kick or strike the black man, but he did see a pool of blood under his head and neck. He (Caldwell) identified Klisz in a lineup and in court as the man with the beard."

Donnie Reynolds, also in the station, saw a black man lying on the floor with one white man standing over him and a fat white man with his right knee on the neck of the black man, who was handcuffed and was hollering, "Get him off of me, help me." When he asked what was wrong, one of the white men said it was police business. He saw blood on the ground and blood coming from the right side of the black man's head and, as he walked toward the stairway, he saw the man who had been kneeling strike the black man in the head four times.

Fritz Knaak was in the station after the White Sox baseball game and saw a black man lying on the floor with a white man sitting on top of him. When the black man hollered for help, the white man told him to "shut up" and hit his head on the cement floor at least five times.

Andrew Laties was walking through the concourse of the station when he heard repeated cries for help and saw a black man lying on his stomach, with a stocky-built white man with a dark moustache next to him and a larger white man with light-colored sideburns squatting on the black man's buttocks. The larger man leaned over the black man and hit him twice with his right hand at the base of the skull and top of the neck. When he told the other white man "to stop that" the man replied, "Keep walking, this is police business." The black man was hit a third time by the same white man, and he (Laties) saw a pool of blood at the black man's head. The black man at that time was prone and was not moving.—*People v. Earullo*, 113 Ill. App. 3d 774, 779 (Ill. App. Ct. 1983). http://casetext.com/case/people-v-earullo

Page 94. "blanket endorsement"
Associated Press, "Jesse Jackson Raps Decision in Slaying Case," *Santa Cruz Sentinel*, December 24, 1981, p. 3.

Page 95. "full tale"
Robert Cooley, with Hillel Levin, *When Corruption Was King: How I Helped the Mob Rule Chicago, Then Brought the Outfit Down* (New York: Carroll & Graf Publishers, 2004) 160-163.

Page 96. "mob payback"
For several years, Judge Cieslik's daughter Debra attempted to restore her father's reputation, utilizing a blog. After her death in 2012, this blog was taken down.

Consider the following two article excerpts through the lens of the profound corruption in Chicago courts, and you can recognize the mob's fingerprints: punishing Cieslik for the Ramey case's verdict and jail sentences.

"The Illinois Courts Commission has reprimanded Cook County Circuit Court Judge Arthur Cieslik for 'disparaging, intemperate, injudicious and rude remarks' that he made to three women attorneys."—Debra Cassens Moss, "Judge Says He's Sorry," *ABA Journal,* October 1, 1987.

"Chief Judge Harry Comerford and all but one Cook County judge seeking retention kept their jobs in an election marked both by the failure of minority groups to oust Comerford and concern that lingering bitterness could affect the nation's largest court system.

Only Arthur Cieslik, who was uniformly targeted by major bar associations and newspapers for abrasive conduct toward women in his courtroom, failed to win the required 60 percent vote necessary to retain his Circuit Court seat."—James Warren and Joseph R. Tybor, "Chief Judge Comerford Retained, Cieslik Ousted," *Chicago Tribune,* November 10, 1988.

5—REFUGEES IN PARIS

Page 103. "school for improvising musicians"
"I was able to establish my own independent program: neurology frontiering on Jungian psychiatry, questioning and analysis.... I based my institute on the Bauhaus: the hippest institution you can imagine, no politics and no nationality involved, a cultural research center to present clear ideas of design and art to the world."—"Alan Silva: Interviews with Dan Warburton," November 8th-22nd 2002, http://paristransatlantic.com/magazine/interviews/silva.html

6—RETURNING THE FAVOR

Page 110. "AACM School"
"The AACM School of Music aims to give talented youth the opportunity to realize his or her musical potential, and to give all students the understanding of the beauty of music in general and Great Black Music in particular. This appreciation in turn, results in a respect for music of all types and a comprehension of the merits of discipline. The AACM School of Music aims to foster the skills and discipline in young people that they can apply to any endeavor they may undertake. The AACM School of Music faculty is made up entirely of AACM members, many of whom are themselves graduates of the program. All teachers volunteer their time and expertise."—AACM website: http://www.aacmchicago.org/school

Page 113. Gertrude Stein, "Ladies Voices," *Geography and Plays* (London: Four Seas: 1916).

Page 117. "I worked in hundreds of schools"
"Founded in 1978, Child's Play Touring Theatre was the first theatre company to realize the value of children's own writing and perform exclusively stories and poems written by young authors. Combining the important, imaginative writings of children with the craftsmanship of professional theatre artists and educators, we created a unique stage where children's voices can be heard, examined and treasured."—Child's Play website: http://www.cptt.org/about_us/index.html

Page 117. "Evening of the Bearded Heart"
From my essay, "Interpreting *Ursonate*":
"Working as a children's theatre actor and improvisor—and as a jazz musician with several bands and under a number of teachers—had helped me learn how to inject my own ideas into any text, even ones like *Ursonate* [also called *Sonata in Primeval Sounds*] with no coherent linguistic meaning. That is, I was interested in using *Ursonate* for my own purposes: as a framework for expressing my own ideas; as a template for the integration of jazz improvisation and theater improvisation."—Andrew Laties, "Andy Laties on Kurt Schwitters and Dada: Interpreting *Ursonate*," Artist Organized Art website: http://artistorganizedart.org/commons/2009/07/andy-laties-on-kurt-schwitters-dada.html (New York: Artist Organized Art, 2009).

Page 118. Ed Sacks, "AACM School small ensemble," photograph (Ed Sacks Photography: Chicago, 1986).

Page 121. "Willing suspension of disbelief"
"…my endeavours should be directed to persons and characters supernatural, or at least romantic; yet so as to transfer from our inward nature a human interest and a semblance of truth sufficient to procure for these shadows of imagination that willing suspension of disbelief for the moment, which constitutes poetic faith." Samuel Taylor Coleridge, *Biographia Literaria,* Chapter XIV (1817).

THE MUSIC THIEF

ANDREW LATIES co-founded Easton Book Festival, Book & Puppet Company, Vox Pop, The Children's Bookstore, Chicago Children's Museum Store, and Eric Carle Museum Bookstore. He shared the 1987 Women's National Book Association's Pannell Award for bringing children and books together. His *Rebel Bookseller: Why Indie Businesses Represent Everything You Want to Fight For—From Free Speech to Buying Local to Building Communities* won the 2006 Independent Publisher Award and is available in a second edition from Seven Stories Press. He recently published *Son of Rebel Bookseller: A Very Large Homework Assignment,* co-written with son Samuel Laties.

www.ingramcontent.com/pod-product-compliance
Lightning Source LLC
Chambersburg PA
CBHW071853070526
44583CB00016B/1674